A Charmed Life

A Charmed Life

The Story of How Red Boots and Cupcakes Can Help You Find Happiness

SHARON MITCHELL

BALBOA.
PRESS
A DIVISION OF HAY HOUSE

Balboa Press books may be ordered through booksellers or by contacting:

Balboa Press
A Division of Hay House
1663 Liberty Drive
Bloomington, IN 47403
www.balboapress.com.au
1-(877) 407-4847

ISBN: 978-1-4525-0289-2 (sc)
ISBN: 978-1-4525-0290-8 (e)

Printed in the United States of America

Balboa Press rev. date: 10/21/2011

To find out more about the author go to :
www.sharonmitchell.com.au

Contents

For Josie and Jackson:
every day I live my amends to you.

Chapter 1

The Gondola Story

(Rock Bottom)

If you know someone who tries to drown their sorrows, tell them that sorrows know how to swim.

—H. Jackson Brown, Jr

At sunset on the day of my fifteenth wedding anniversary, I sat in a beautifully restored gondola on the Swan River in Western Australia.

As the gondolier quietly pushed us across the smooth, calm water, soft music played in the background generated from a small CD player behind him. My husband sat close beside me as we sipped champagne and ate slowly from the platter of delicacies displayed artistically on the silver tray in front of us.

We had flown to Western Australia from the eastern states earlier in the week. Our children were with our babysitter back at the five-star hotel we had booked for the duration of our holiday.

My husband had meticulously planned the remainder of our evening. He had booked us into Perth's best hotel. I found out later that he had arranged for the room to be full of bunches of red roses, with rose petals covering the floor and bed. He had planned that after our gondola ride, we were to eat a five-course dinner at one of Perth's most sought-after restaurants.

For anyone looking on at this scene, everything in my life might have seemed perfect.

Through our eighteen-year relationship, fifteen of which we were married, my husband and I accumulated everything I had ever wished for. We had two beautiful, healthy children—eleven-year-old twins. A pigeon pair, boy/girl set, first grandchildren to both sides of our family. Both children attended a private school close to our home. We owned a multimillion-dollar business in a booming economy with nothing but an excellent economic outlook ahead of us. We owned a large multi-storey house on the hill in one of Canberra's prestigious northern suburbs, and three late-model European cars—including the coveted red convertible—sat shining in our garage.

And then, right there, my life flashed before my eyes. As I sat in the gondola, the soft breeze blowing against my face and the setting sun warming me, I realized, in that one split second, that I no longer wanted for anything. I finally had everything I had ever worked for. I actually had it all. This was *it*. As good as it gets, I had the whole fairytale ending.

And I was so unhappy I could have died.

Why, since I had everything that our society had told me to work for since I was a very little girl, was I not happy? This was not at all what I had expected it to be. I had expected when I finally had it all that I would at last be happy.

And so suddenly, for the first time in my life, I was without hope.

Right up until that time, every minute of my life until now, I had always had hope that one day I *would* be happy—one day.

One of my earliest memories is when I was five, when my father left us. I don't remember there being any fighting. I don't even know if there was any; I just remember us being alone.

My mum, older brother, younger brother, and I left the small country town where we then lived and moved to Canberra, or rather Queanbeyan, the small town right next to Canberra. It offered cheaper rents for a poor, single-parent family.

My mother got a job quite quickly at the post office of Parliament House in Canberra, but an entry-level job in the public service does not bring a large income, and we were poor. I'm not really sure when it occurred to me that we were poor, but I do know that I was pretty sure of it by the time Christmas came that year. My mother had already tried to soften the blow of an empty Christmas by warning us that there was no extra money for presents or Christmas food. Then on Christmas Eve we were all surprised when the knock on the door saw us welcoming in an officer of the Salvation Army. He was carrying a box with just one present for each of us three kids and Christmas lunch for the next day. Now, I use the term 'Christmas lunch' loosely, as the ham came in a tin. But I know we savoured that lunch and every inch of that ham, and I still have the small faux opal necklace that was my present that day. And to this day, I donate freely to the Salvation Army. I will never forget what they did for us.

That was the day that I knew we were poor. And I decided then that I knew the two things you needed to be happy.

The root of my problems, I believed, were no father and no money.

So, a marriage that lasted and money: that was what I understood I needed to be happy. I knew right then what my goal was to be. I would get married, stay married, and get lots and lots of money. That would bring happiness. I never wanted a knight in shining armour to bring me all this; I was willing to work for it and that's what I intended to do.

And so, here I was in the gondola about thirty-three years later, and everything I had worked for had *not* bought the happiness I expected.

However, on that day I was not ready to admit to myself or anyone else that this could be because I was drunk.

I was always drunk.

I had my first drink at fifteen years old during a party my mum and stepdad were having. My best friend and I topped up our glasses of lemonade with port from stepdad's port barrel. I loved it. *Loved it.* I believe that a non-alcoholic cannot quite understand the feeling we alcoholics get when we have our first drink. It is literally heaven. Nothing, nothing gives you that feeling like the first mouthful as the warmth spreads through your body, and you know that the oblivion will soon blank your mind. We never drink for the flavour. We never drink to be social. We drink for oblivion, numbness, and to dull our feelings. I wanted nothing else but to drink, and it took only a few short nights before my friends and I were down by the trees at the school oval after dark sculling from the wine casks. I got drunk that next time, and every single time I drank after that. Every single time I drank for the rest of my life I would get drunk. I have never, ever, had just one glass of wine. Never.

It only took a couple of months and I was drinking every night. By the time I was in year eleven, the arguments with my mum and stepdad were excessive, and of course got in the way of my drinking. I got a government flat to live in, as it was the only place I could afford, left school and got a job behind the counter at the local department store.

Apart from my drinking, I really only had one thing I was interested in—decorating cakes. I was lucky enough to get an apprenticeship as a pastry chef, as I knew this was the qualification I would need if I wanted to make some money out of my cake decorating. Unfortunately, what I did not know is that pastry chefs start work about three in the morning. Since I was out until about 3 a.m. every night drinking, it became very difficult to work. I went to work still drunk, and I lived on a supply of No-Doze.

I gave up my dream of becoming a cake decorator and found a job as a bookkeeper. This was the best job I could get as a young, unqualified alcoholic in the making. It was about this time that an incident in my government flats made me realize it was time for a change.

Now, this was before the events at Port Arthur, and therefore before Australia's strong gun laws. One night, as I was coming home from after-work drinks with my workmates, my upstairs neighbour, who

obviously had a mental illness of some kind, became angry, began
screaming, and ended up wielding a loaded gun right at me!

At that point, I knew if I did not make some changes I was not going
to get the marriage and family I wanted, or the money I needed to
make me happy.

I now know that many alcoholics are quite high achievers and that
we can often manage not only to achieve what 'normal' people do,
but sometimes even a bit more. And all with a raging hangover. So,
every day for the next twenty years, with a hangover that should
flatten an elephant, I got up and worked my ass off in an attempt to
get what I wanted.

On top of the need for a safer place to live, I was in need of a bigger
goal. I decided that a prestigious car was a good sign of wealth and
happiness, so I set my sights on an E36 318 BMW—Boston green.
On the mirror in my bedroom, in red lipstick, I wrote:

BMW 10-3-1999

My goal was the car, and the date was my thirtieth birthday.

When I met Simon, my one-day-to-be-husband, I was twenty. I let
him know that this life was what I was working for. I remember
when I said to him, 'If you stick with me, you'd better hang on for
the ride, because I want to make a fortune.'

He also liked the idea of money, and therefore happiness, and he
was willing to join in. We were like two sides of a piece of Velcro,
we stuck together so firmly, everywhere always together, working,
working for this goal of ours. And I always had a raging hangover.
And I'm not sure where love fitted into that equation either.

And so it was at this time that, unknown to me, my other big
'addiction' started to grow. I was a codependent in the making,

and my relationship with Simon was the perfect environment to breed this painful, painful condition. Codependency is a debilitating condition that drained me of my self-esteem, my potential, and my very soul.

When I got pregnant with our twins, Josie and Jackson, I did manage to stop drinking for that nine months. It was the only time in my adult life that I did not drink. I hated not drinking. I 'white knuckled' through that time, and after my twins were born, I was still sitting on the bed in the labour ward, my legs still too numb from the epidural to walk, when I had my first drink in my hand. And so it began again.

It was when my twins were newborns that I decided that it was still okay to be a parent and drink this much if I only drank at night time. Night time for me was 6 p.m., so 6 p.m every night is when it would start. I would wait, with an un-moveable strictness, for my 6 p.m start. Best, best moment of my day. Every day. And then I would hate every moment of the night after that as I slowly (and not so slowly) drank my way to oblivion. I thought I was still doing my part as a parent as long as I got my kids to bed before I fell into a drunken, unwakeable stupor.

For some reason, I told myself very early on that I would never drink and drive. And I never did. I was quite ingenious in finding ways for other people to drive for me, but nevertheless, I never did drink and drive, and this is one stupid thing I do not have to regret.

Amazingly, while I was doing all this drinking, I was still the primary caregiver for my kids, and I was also working to bring in some money. Simon had to finish his accounting degree, and so I had to earn some money. Then we bought into a business that was initially not profitable at all. I would do bookkeeping work in between looking after the kids in order to pay the bills over that time. In the financial year of our children's first year on earth, my husband and

I earned a combined income of twelve thousand dollars. We were a long, long way from my goal.

Over time, the business became more successful, and four months before my thirtieth birthday, I became the very proud owner of a Boston green E36 318 BMW. Now I could see that our goals were achievable, and so we continued to work towards that goal of happiness that came with financial security.

However, during these years, my codependency was starting to cripple me emotionally. All I ever wanted to do was make my husband and children happy. I believed that their happiness would become my happiness. I didn't want them to feel any pain, physically or emotionally; I just wanted them to be happy. I would provide for Simon's happiness before everything else in my life. Simon never had to threaten me; he never had to bully me. Whatever he wanted, or I even thought he wanted, I would provide. It is very, very exhausting to be responsible for the happiness of three other human beings, and of course, it is an unachievable goal. And in the process of trying to provide everything to Simon and the kids, I completely, wholly, and entirely lost any last piece of my 'self'.

Over these years, as my drinking had progressively got worse, Simon adapted to my excessive drinking, believing it to be a part of who I was. He knew that I suffered a lot of anxiety, and he knew that I self-medicated with alcohol. To a large extent, it was the 'elephant in the room' of our relationship. It was the thing that we never really talked about as long as I kept providing what was required of me in the relationship as a wife and mother. I could easily drink such enormous amounts of alcohol that it would have flattened an elephant, but as long as I continued to be a functioning wife and mother, which I did most of the time, then this particular elephant would not get discussed.

Although Josie and Jackson were still young, up until this time, to some extent, they also accepted my drinking as part of who I was. As

I was such an over-functioning alcoholic, they both knew that they could still rely on me to provide for them. In a physical capacity, I never let them down; they were always fed and clothed, always at the right place at the right time. Always. Unfortunately though, the anger and unhappiness I lived with during my drinking are what they primarily remember from my time as an actively alcoholic mother. It took all my energy, both emotional and physical, managing everything, for everyone, all day, every day. I had absolutely nothing left for feelings, I had nothing left for joy, and I had nothing else left to give my children, even if I'd known they needed it. I was very angry at myself and my addiction, and that anger radiated itself to everyone around me, including my children.

And so, after all those years of working on making a happy marriage through providing every need to my husband and making lots of money through working hard and taking risks, I sat there in that gondola, unhappy and unfulfilled.

I then did what I always did when I could not identify why I was unhappy: I drank some more.

After the gondola ride, we did go to dinner at the restaurant; I don't remember any of it. Later that night, Simon called an ambulance to the hotel, as I was in so much pain from what I now know was my inflamed liver. Simon was still not ready to admit that these problems were caused by my excessive alcohol consumption.

After they gave me painkillers, I slept, we woke up, and I just started drinking again.

Something in me the day before had clicked, and I no longer had any reason to keep trying anymore, and so on this day, my alcoholism took its final hold on me. I could not, just could not, stop drinking. Now I was past trying to numb these feelings of hopelessness, and my drinking was just a matter of getting more alcohol into me. I'm not sure I can explain how it feels for your whole body—every cell—to be begging, begging to get another drink into it. All day, every day.

It was three months from the May of my fifteenth wedding anniversary to the August when I finally hit rock bottom. Those three months were hell.

I slept with alcohol next to my bed; as soon as I woke up, I drank. Then I drank all day, every day. I was in so much pain as my body slowly shut down. I was long beyond the point of eating any food to speak of. Every now and again, my children would try to get me to eat something, but my body would throw the food up straight away. I threw up all the time though, food or no food. I was poisoning my body so badly with the amount of alcohol I was consuming that as fast as I drank, my body was trying to get rid of it.

I was injuring myself all the time, as you do when your body is incapable of functioning any longer. I was regularly bruised and broken, with sprained ankles so regular that I was on crutches on numerous occasions.

In one of my last trips outside the house during this time, my mother took me to the mall to go shopping. Whilst in the mall, I suffered an alcoholic seizure. One thing a lot of people do not know is that you can actually die from alcohol withdrawal. So, I had been in the mall about an hour, and even though I did have alcohol with me in my trusty water bottle—I thought people would think it was water—I was not drinking as much as I would have had I been at home. Even though I was still drunk, my body was going into withdrawal, as I was not *as* drunk as I normally was.

So, the ambulance was again called, and they stabilised me and told my mum and husband (who had been called by then) that I needed to go to the hospital. Of course, I would not be taken, as I thought I knew what they were going to say . . . .

Even worse than any physical pain during this time was the emotional pain. I was suffering alcoholic hallucinations, which are horrific. They are very real, very scary, and unavoidable, as they appear everywhere and anywhere, so there is no escape from what is your worst nightmare. Mine came in the form of snakes. Anywhere in my home (as I rarely left the house by this time), they would appear and attack me, biting me. The pain seemed so real and so intense and was unavoidable. I drank more to get short spaces of oblivion between the physical and emotional pain.

Even worse, and actually the worst thing that ever happened to me during my active alcoholism, were the blackouts. By this time, nearly my whole life was lived in a blackout. I only have small snippets of my life during this time as I came in and out of the blackouts. I am not sure I can explain what it is like to come out of a blackout and have absolutely no recollection of what you have done or to whom. I knew I was angry at my life, my addiction, and myself. I never knew if I ever acted on this anger when I was in a blackout. There is nothing, nothing, worse than when I came out of a blackout and the first thing that would come to my mind was, *Have I injured my children? Have I killed one of them?*

I remember that when I was a kid, I could not understand why someone would commit suicide. I thought that if your life was so bad that you wanted to kill yourself, you would just get on a bus and go to a new town. Leave the people and things that were making you so sad and just start up life anew. What I did not understand at the time is that the worst things that happen to us all happen in our minds; they are our feelings and our emotional pain. And no matter where we go, we cannot get away from those feelings. That is why we kill ourselves.

I did not have the courage to kill myself. But as I was absolutely hopeless, I really wanted to die.

On my last time outside the house during my active addiction, we met with family friends for lunch. Simon was, until this time, still of the opinion that my 'illness' was related to my anxieties and would eventually get better, so he was attempting to carry on as normal. As I was still living much of my life in a blackout, I only remember a small snippet of being at the lunch and then all I remember is being in hospital. I had suffered another alcoholic seizure, but this time, it was in front of our family friends. Simon was no longer able to avoid the 'elephant in the room', and he drove me to hospital.

As I came in and out of consciousness, I remember some of the things the doctors told me. First, I remember the doctor who told me, 'You need to stop drinking.' Of course I was not fit to answer him, but I remember thinking what an absolutely ridiculous thing this was to say. Did he know nothing about drinking? Didn't he know I would do anything to stop drinking? Didn't he know that there was nothing, nothing I could do to stop drinking? It was beyond my capabilities. Every cell in my body screamed out for a drink, every minute of every day.

And then I do remember what the next doctor told me. 'Sharon, your body is shutting down. Your liver is about to fail. This is going to kill you, not later but sooner. We do not put active alcoholics on a transplant list.'

This was the first time anyone had told me I was an alcoholic, and he had told me I would probably die.

They said they would put me in the detox unit attached to the hospital. It was a matter of responsibility, but they did not expect that my body would recover.

And so, my journey began.

Thank God, I did survive without my body shutting down, and I have never had a drink since that morning I was taken into detox.

It began a journey that has made me the person I have become today. Once I detoxed through the physical pain of alcohol withdrawal, I then went on to the enormous emotional journey of recovery. For me, this has not only been a recovery from alcoholism, but a recovery from the shadow of a human being I had become that day on the gondola.

One of the important things that I have found out during this journey is that the universe or God (whichever you prefer to choose to believe in) will always try to teach you lessons. First, the universe will start throwing pebbles of wisdom at you to make you see each lesson you need to learn. If you continue to ignore each of the pebbles, then eventually, in order to really get your attention, the universe will throw a *whole stone wall*. Here's my first word of wisdom to you: a pebble hurts much less than a whole stone wall. When the universe throws a pebble at you, listen, and listen good.

During my journey, I feel that I have been taught lots of lessons. Some of these lessons are absolutely life-changing, but all of them are important for us to learn at some stage in our life's journey. Take whichever pebbles are useful to you from my journey, and you too can allow them to change your life.

In this book, I share with you some of the many, many things that I have learned during this journey, each lesson is presented as the charm on my charm bracelet of life. At the back of this book, I have included a list of books that I recommend you read to find out more on any of the lessons that I share with you in my story. In my journey, everything I have learned has given me back one thing I lost that day on the gondola—*hope*. I wish the same for you.

Charm 1:

*Admitting the need for change is
the first step on our journey.*

Chapter 2

The Dinosaur Eggs

(Feelings)

Sometimes my feelings are so hot that I have to take the pen and put them out on paper to keep me from setting me afire inside.

—Mark Twain

My admission into the detox unit was, until that time, the scariest thing I had done in my life. Simon and my kids took me up to the unit early in the morning of the 14th August. I had been taken home in between that last visit to emergency and this admission to the detox unit. The doctors had told Simon, and my mum, not to allow me to stop drinking until I got back to the detox unit. If I stopped, or even cut down my drinking too much, I would suffer another seizure. The doctors would need to medicate me and keep me in a medically supervised environment when my body went into the full detox process.

As we left the house on that morning, I remember taking my last drink. Simon and the kids had walked through to the front of the house towards the car, and they were out of sight. I had obviously continued to drink through the night and then as soon as I woke up that morning. This was just one last drink to get me through the trip to the hospital, which was twenty minutes away. I grabbed a large tumbler from the cupboard, drained the wine from one of the large four-litre casks that always filled the bulk of the shelf space in the double-door fridge, and topped the tumbler to the brim. I then swallowed and gulped that golden liquid as quickly as my throat would allow. I look back now and realize what an unceremonious end that was to my long, and stellar, drinking career. Should I have spent three minutes to pop the cork on a bottle of vintage champagne and savour each bubble to the end? No, for me it was all about the effect. The drug. It was all about the numbness. And so my last glass was sculled, and I shuffled to the front door and off into the unknown world of recovery.

On that crisp winter morning, the detox unit was warm, but grey. Very grey. Simon, Josie, Jackson, and I were taken into a small room on the bottom floor of the detox unit to say our goodbyes. Not surprisingly, I was suddenly so fearful of what was about to happen to me that I wanted to run and escape. I told my family and the staff how I felt in no uncertain terms. Looking back now, I see that probably every person who is going into the unit attempts to escape at the last minute. So I guess they are very practiced at saying whatever they need to in order to get the alcoholic to stay. I don't remember everything they said to me; I was still quite drunk at this stage. I do remember they said that it would not hurt, but it did. I remember they said I could leave whenever I wanted, but I couldn't; and I remember they said they would let me talk to my family whenever I wanted, but they didn't. I don't hold any anger towards the staff at the detox unit now because I realize that you cannot, and should not, rationalize with a drunk who is drunk.

After I had cried copious tears and said goodbye to my connections to the outside world, they took me straight up to my room. My room was to be right next to the nurses' station so that they could keep a close eye on me. You see, not everyone goes into the detox unit drunk, and hardly anyone goes in quite as drunk as I was. So they knew that when my body detoxed, it was going to be bad. Some patients who enter detox realize that they have a problem and don't know how to fix it, but they don't necessarily drink every day. Even those who do drink every day don't always drink all day, every day. I had the honour of being the drunkest of the drunks. I'm sure this is not something I had aspired to in my fifth grade essay titled 'What I Want to Be When I Grow Up'.

My room was sparse, with just a bed, bedside table, and bathroom. There was nothing like a radio or TV. I initially thought this was strange, but I had no idea that within hours I would be in pain so great that entertainment would be the last thing on my mind. And then they opened my suitcase and started to go through everything I had brought with me. They were looking for any hidden alcohol or drugs and even confiscated any toiletry items that contained alcohol. I was surprised that this included not only the removal of obvious items including alcohol, like mouthwash, but others that were less obvious, like some shampoos that just had small amounts of the drug. Whilst I thought this was strange at the time, I was about to see how desperate we, the patients of the detox unit, would become to get our next drink.

The final part of my induction into the unit involved needles. They took me to a small area off one of the corridors. It wasn't a room, as such; it was a kind of alcove. There was no door and no privacy. I sat on the grey, vinyl-covered chair. They drew blood for a blood alcohol test. I don't remember if they actually told me what the result was, but I do remember the gasp from one nurse to the other as they declared, 'This women should be dead. That is a lot of alcohol.' They knew for sure then that my detox was going to be painful. They explained to me that they would continue to take blood alcohol tests a couple of times a day until I was down to zero. They then went on to give me what I thought then was a painful shot of vitamin B12, to start replacing what was lost during my drinking. I didn't know that a lot worse was still to come.

So by this time, it had been perhaps just over an hour since that last drink at home, and I was starting to feel it. I started to shake and to feel very uncomfortable. They took me to my room and said I needed to lie down. At that time, I thought that might help in some way. It didn't, and nothing did. As I went into that room, I did not realize that I would be unable to leave it for eight long and painful days. And so the detox began. Even though they medicated me, the feeling of discomfort went to a feeling like nothing I had ever experienced before. My skin was crawling, I was shivering, and every cell in my body was crying out for the alcohol that I knew would make this stop. And then the pain began. Every part of my body was aching, stabbing, and prickling. It felt like the worst physical pain that could be inflicted on me, but it was coming from inside of me, under my skin, and inside my body. The ache of the pain was so great that it encompassed me, so that the whole outside world, outside my room, and even outside the space of my own mind, became irrelevant. I focused on taking each breath, one tiny gasp at a time.

I lost the ability to stand, or even to sit up. I could not even *move* my legs. My arms and hands did not even have the ability to grasp a cup to sip water. My whole body shuddered with the shakes of an addict in withdrawal. I just lay, shaking, without sleep, but with pain, so much pain, and the one thing I knew would take this all away from me was no longer within my reach. My drug was my alcohol. For so many years, I had seen it as my steadfast friend who had solved all my problems, covered all my errors, and cured all my woes; now I must pay the price. Now I was paying for my inability to deal with each of those problems, errors, and woes as they had appeared to me, choosing instead to use my alcohol to deal with each of those trials as they happened.

The nurses continued to test my blood for its alcohol content over the first few days of my stay, and it was on 16th August, two days after my admission, that my blood alcohol was finally down to zero. Some people make their sobriety 'birthday' on the date of their last drink; I decided to make mine on the 16th August, as this was the first day I was actually sober, but two days after the date of my last drink. In many ways, this date is more important than my 'belly button' birthday (the anniversary of the day I was born). It doesn't actually take that much to turn a year older, but it certainly takes a lot to stay another year sober.

For more than a week, I lay there in this continued state of physical pain and emotional despair, and then slowly, very slowly, I began to gain some control over my body. I was still shaking so badly that I could not hold a cup still enough to drink from it, but with the aid of a straw, I began to sip water. And then eventually, I could sit up and swing my legs off the end of the bed. The possibility of sleep for more than minutes at a time became an option, and the nurses brought relaxation music into the room, allowing me to sleep sometimes an hour or more at a time. And then, on the morning of my eighth day in the detox unit, I took my first sober steps.

Very slowly, I shuffled (because that's all I could manage) to the bathroom. I was going to have my first shower, but it was unbelievably bad. To this day, I remember so clearly how I felt standing in the shower, my legs so weak I was barely able to stand, and in the end, I was only able to stay upright for not more than a couple of minutes.

I felt I had lost control of my body, even though I was now finally beginning to get control of my mind. I stood in the shower that day and vowed to myself, *I will never, ever go through this again.*

For me, to drink again is to die.

On my ninth day in the detox unit, a long-time sober alcoholic came in to chat to me in the recovery unit. He was old, and he was a man, and this was the first time I had ever met a person who told me that he was an alcoholic. I had never met one before—or at least, not one who had ever admitted it to me. His name was Stan, and he told me this was going to be the hardest, most painful time in my life, and that I had no idea at all. We sat and chatted that Tuesday night in quiet tones in the corner of the common room of the unit. Stan was there to speak with anyone who was willing or wanted to hear what he had to say. I now know that sober alcoholics are willing to help other suffering alcoholics when the alcoholics are willing to listen and to learn. I must have looked desperate enough, because Stan made a beeline for the seat next to me. I drank my tea through a straw, the half-filled cup still shaky in my hands, but this was something Stan was used to seeing in us 'newcomers'. I listened to what he had to say.

He said there was help for me. He said there were a lot of people who were just like me who would partner me through this journey of recovery. There had been many, many people like me who had passed in and out these doors of detox. Some had drunk again and end ended up dead. Some had stayed momentarily sober and then drunk again to end up back in detox, each time the doors getting a little bit smaller and a little bit harder to get through. But he assured me that there were many, many people who had had the tools of recovery laid at their feet, picked up those tools, and gone on to live healthy, happy lives of long-term sobriety.

Thank God that on that night, I decided to pick up the tools. Stan said, 'Sharon, you may leave this room tonight and never drink again.'

If someone had told me, as they took me into detox, what I would have to go through in order to get some good quality recovery, I absolutely would not have gone into the unit. I would not have begun the journey. Even though my other option was death, I still, one hundred percent, would not have gone into that unit. I would have chosen death.

At that time, I was a grey shadow of a person, incapable of even imagining that I had the ability to grow, to change, to improve, or to offer anything to the world. What was the point in me trying to get any kind of recovery?

But the day that Stan came into the unit to speak with me was the day that I was handed back my hope. He said, 'Sharon, you will need to accept that you are powerless over alcohol. You will need to find a power greater than yourself, and you will need to make amends to those whom you have injured though your drinking.' And right then, I knew what I had to do to make amends to my children, who were the most injured and most important people in my life. I knew that I would need to get sober and stay sober in order to live my amends to my children. Every day I stayed sober, from this day forward, would be my living amends to Josie and Jackson.

So I started to speak to other alcoholics, some just newly recovered. Even more importantly, I started listening to some alcoholics who had been sober a long time.

I discovered that there were a number of key changes they had made in their lives. One of the first and most important of these was to learn how to feel my feelings.

I was completely enlightened to hear about this concept.

I thought that I already had been feeling my feelings. I thought that the anger, fear, and guilt that I lived with were all the feelings that the world had to offer, and I thought I was feeling them a lot.

What I did not realize was that I had been using my alcohol consumption to numb my feelings for so many years that I no longer knew, or maybe I never had known, what it was to feel true, raw feelings.

I now know that we all distract ourselves from feeling our feelings all the time. For some of us, it is clear to the outside world that we are not dealing with our feelings—those of us who drink or drug. But what about everyone else? I believe that our society does not generally teach us to feel our feelings—it teaches us to 'deal with' our feelings, as if they are something that we are meant to avoid.

Why do we do that? Why do we want to make our feelings go away? I see many other people, who are not alcoholics, who also do whatever they have to do to get rid of those feelings and manage their anxieties. Food addicts, bulimics, anorexics, workaholics, over-exercisers, gamblers, shopaholics, control freaks, those who over-parent, codependents, love and sex addicts, cutters, drug addicts (both illegal and prescription), obsessive gamers, porn addicts, and computer over-users. Anything and everything we will use to distract ourselves from acknowledging our feelings.

And don't think it's not you, because everyone uses one or more of these things, to some level, to manage their anxieties and protect themselves from feeling their feelings.

When was the last time you sat? Just sat? No TV, no conversation, no music to listen to, no book or even magazine—just sat with your feelings and let yourself feel? You probably have not done this for a very, very long time, if ever. Try it, and see what feeling comes up. See what feeling or feelings are sitting there, feelings that you have probably been avoiding.

When I first realized the importance of allowing myself to feel, I was told that this process was going to hurt, and hurt it did.

I call it the ripe tomato experience.

On my first day un-medicated and out of detox, every feeling came at me like nothing I had ever felt before in my adult life. I felt an overwhelming burst of feelings pushing themselves onto me so quickly and forcefully that I could not even begin to process names for each feeling. Each feeling came at me like a hot needle pushing into my consciousness, like the feeling of hot boiling water as it peels the skin off a fresh, ripe tomato.

But I did not pick up a drink to numb those feelings. I did scream and cry and allow myself to feel each feeling. I did not try to take away any feelings, or even process them or fix them or change them. I just felt them.

I continued to feel those feelings, unaided by any kind of relief, day in and day out, and it did get easier. After time, the ripe tomato feeling went away, and I started to learn the ability to name the feelings I was having. I still didn't try to cover them or take them away. I could then begin to process those feelings, and at some level, I began to discover why I was feeling each of those feelings.

Along the way, I learnt that you do not have to take a feeling away just because you don't like it. You can just let the feeling happen. I am not saying that this was easy, but each time I just sat with an uncomfortable feeling, it was just a little bit easier to feel next time.

I was also very aware from quite early on that even though I could not pick up a drink or a drug, I could also not cover my feelings with any type of relief; I would just need to feel the feeling. I was very scared of some kind of addiction transfer where I would stop covering my feelings with one thing and cover them with another.

Going from one addiction to another is known as 'swapping the witch for the bitch', and I knew I needed to avoid it. If you stop eating chocolate but take up smoking, you have just swapped the witch for the bitch. Feel the feeling instead.

I knew I had learned this lesson when we were on holiday in London during my recovery. I had been told about a particular shoe shop in London where I could find the most amazing red boots ever. Now, I love a pair of nice red boots as much as the next girl, so I was very excited to take a relatively empty suitcase with me to the UK so that I could buy these boots and bring them home. The highly anticipated day of purchasing the boots arrived, and it did not take long before Simon and I were in the midst of a nice, big argument. Nothing to do with the boots, just a regular, run-of-the-mill, codependent argument. As I marched out the door of the hotel, I was feeling all types of emotions and feelings, and I knew that I would feel better when I went and bought the boots. I also knew that if I bought the boots right now, I would be swapping the witch for the bitch, making myself feel better by avoiding these feelings of anxiety. I would not be allowing myself to just *feel*. So I did *not* go and buy the red boots; I just felt the feelings and added some emotional growth to my repertoire. As it happens, God must have thought those boots should be part of my journey, because a few days later, I was given the opportunity to be back near the coveted shoe store. I did buy those beautiful red boots, and I wear them proudly now as my reminder to myself of how important it is to feel those feelings every time.

I was active in finding more feelings that I had previously been afraid to face. I was starting to see how great it was when I had a feeling and I pushed my way through the fear and into the solution.

I describe this as the dinosaur egg experience.

That was because every time I would feel an unwanted or unexpected feeling, I felt like I was a baby dinosaur breaking out of my egg for the first time. I would scratch and bleed (metaphorically speaking), and it would hurt (no metaphor, it would really hurt), but once I had broken through the shell, the sunshine on the outside would be bright and warm and well worth the pain. And each time, I could see that some kind of new opportunity in life would be on offer for me.

So, this lesson is clear.

Don't try to get rid of your feelings, don't feel you have failed by having those feelings, and don't try to take them away.

Just feel your feelings. Just let them happen. It really is that simple.

Now, a word of warning here about letting your feelings take you over or wallowing in your sad feelings. It is great to feel your feelings, but you have to know when to feel them and when let them go.

When I feel sad, lonely, or inadequate, I like to wrap the blanket of sadness around me. I surround myself with it, and that blanket of sadness feels so warm and somehow comforting. Then I want to take myself, wrapped in my warm sadness blanket, and step into a deep, dark metaphorical hole. I want to sit in the warm, dark hole with my comforting blanket of sadness wrapped around me.

The problem is that if I allow myself to go down the sadness hole, I find it very hard to get myself back up again. Once I want to get out, to see the light again, it is *too* far up, and it is so hard to climb back out into the light.

What I have learnt to do when I feel sad is to allow myself to wrap the blanket of sadness around me, but all I ever do is walk over to the hole and look in. I see how dark it is and how deep the hole is, and I remember how hard it is to get out. I stand on the edge, wrapped in the blanket, and *just look* down the hole, but I don't get into the hole. Do not go down the hole of sadness; just look in, but stay up in the light.

So my journey that began inside the grey walls of the detox unit has shown me that feeling our feelings is the first step, and perhaps the most important step, on the journey towards understanding so much more.

Charm 2:

Don't manage your feelings—
experience them.

Chapter 3

Growing Wings

(Fear)

Do the thing you fear, and the death of fear is certain.

—Ralph Waldo Emerson

On the day I was discharged from the detox unit, I was led towards the exit door at the bottom of the building. This door was quite well hidden, and you would not be able to find it unless you were really looking for it. The detox unit was a 'secure unit' and was well fortified to prevent any of the patients (inmates) from trying to leave (escape) during the difficult parts of their detox process. But my day had finally arrived, and I was bursting to get out. I was still quite slow on my feet, so there was no running or jumping involved, but I feel sure that the beaming smile on my face let Simon and the kids know how happy I was to be out of there as they met me on the other side of the door.

The crisp air of a late August Canberra morning hit me as the sunshine touched my face. I squeezed the breath out of Josie and Jackson with my first sober cuddle and didn't even stop to enjoy the open air as I rushed to the car, keen to get on with my first sober day. I was certain life could only get better, expecting not a bump in the road from here on in. *Ahhh,* I thought, *for sure, the hard part is over.*

We drove home, and I walked into our house and down the long entrance corridor to the main part of the house. My walking pace, as I headed further into the house, slowed considerably. My heart sank as the hope I had felt just moments before disappeared, and I was suddenly hit with an all-encompassing feeling of fear. I had just walked back into my own private hell.

When I had been in the detox unit, speaking to Stan and the other recovering alcoholics, they had given me one *big* tip for staying sober. It was to stay away from places where I would drink, to stay away from my drinking destinations of choice, including clubs, pubs, and other regular drinking venues. But I had just walked into my home, the place that should have been my 'safe place', and I immediately realized that this *was* the place I had done most of my drinking. In fact, at the end my drinking, it had been the *only* place for my drinking. This had been my destination for pain and torment—my own personal prison.

I had nowhere to escape, nowhere to be safe. I had nothing between me and the constant reminder of how much my body still wanted to numb itself with a drink. I was very, very scared.

I had been living in fear for a long time, but now, and here on my first sober day in the real world, I realized that I did not know how to live any other way.

I now know that active alcoholism affects the chemicals in your brain so much that fear is a very common side effect of addiction. For this reason, towards the end of my drinking, I was suffering alcoholic hallucinations at home and debilitating panic attacks when I went out. And so, I often self-medicated my anxiety attacks with alcohol, and I left the house less and less. Eventually, I hardly left the house at all, and when I did, I was very, very drunk.

I understand how horrific it feels to live with constant fear. It was like a prison in my mind that I could never escape. I was so fearful that I literally could not think straight. It was physically painful to be in so much fear all the time. Fear was about the only feeling I had left, and I was feeling a lot of it.

Fear ruled my life.

I was fearful of hurting my kids. I was fearful of the pain in my body, which was getting worse by the day. I was fearful of losing my marriage. I was fearful of my life never being any different. I was fearful that people would find out about my drinking and how bad it was. I was fearful of the thoughts in my head and my inability to get away from them.

And so here I was, now newly sober. I no longer had the alcohol, and therefore the chemical changes in my brain, to blame for my fear, but I was still very, very full of fear. Why? Because I had no other basis on which to live my life. I only knew how to live in fear. It was the axis on which all other parts of my life had circled. It was my default position for everything in my life.

So right then, as I stood in my kitchen, sober for the first time, I knew that I would need to find a new basis for life. I needed a new life without fear at its core.

So, the first sober day for me was like it is for so many who are living life without their drug of choice for the first time. You may have heard the term 'one day at a time', which is often used in recovery circles as a means to explain that we each just need to survive through today and then worry about tomorrow when it comes. But unfortunately, on your first day sober, one day seems like a very long time to go without a drink. So, in order to stay sober, many of us, including myself, needed to live minute by minute. That was how I lived through my first day and many more after it. Just one minute at a time, my body screaming all the while for the alcohol which it still believed that it needed to function through the next minute.

On the evening of my first night at home from detox, Simon and I sat in the large Jacuzzi in the indoor spa room of our house. I remember we were talking about the future and what would happen from here on. It was at that time that I had a real light-bulb moment about how much I really did not know about living life sober. I explained to Simon that one of my greatest fears was that even though I was sober, I was essentially still a shell of a human being—a shadow with no true identity of my own and definitely without the ability to hold conversations, act, and interact with other people when I was sober. I decided on that night that the first thing I needed to do was to learn how to *talk* to people, and hopefully in the end I would learn how to do it without fear. Maybe one day I would even live without fear ruling my life.

So, early the next morning, I went and had coffee with some other recovering alcoholics. I was keen to speak to them about how they had lived with the constant fear that I lived in and how they had learned to *live* sober. I parked the car, still excited at the blessing of being sober enough to drive a car. Now much quicker on my feet, I almost skipped into the open-all-hours café/restaurant to meet with these people who would soon become my friends. We huddled around a small table in the back corner of the room, and they told me of some great ways to start living with my fear. A large part of that was to start dealing with the train-wreck of emotions that had been left untouched during my drinking years. I would need to deal with my own emotions and fears and also the pain I had caused to other people during my years of drinking. And I would need to learn how to talk to people sober, and this group of drunks, just like me, was a great place to start. They were tolerant, open-minded, and very understanding. It was like a kindergarten baby-step towards talking and dealing with all the other people in my life.

I continued to meet regularly with these friends, but it was still early in recovery for me. Soon, I realized that although I had begun to start feeling my feelings and I was trying to be less fearful every day, it was still very slow going. I was still so *scared*. It was nothing complicated, nothing new; I just didn't know how to feel fear and let it go.

I realized that emotional freedom was going to be elusive until I ridded myself of the prison that fear had created in my mind.

So I hatched a plan. I realized that not only was I literally living in fear of my emotions, of people, of my thoughts, of the future, but I was actually also fearful of the *physical world*. I was afraid of *things*. I decided that if I was able to overcome some of my biggest physical fears, I would be able to really make some progress towards overcoming all these emotional fears that were holding me back.

My biggest physical fear was aeroplanes, so I decided to go out and learn how to fly a plane.

Yes, *learn how to fly a plane.*

Once I had made the decision to learn how to fly a plane, my fear got even worse. Here I was, only months sober and about to undertake something that even the sanest person would be rightfully fearful of undertaking.

I turned up at the airport on that day of my first lesson full of apprehension. I was literally shaking from head to toe. Absolutely petrified.

My instructor talked me through what to expect in our first lesson. As we walked out to the plane, the thing that hit me first was how *tiny* these planes are. 'You won't really need your jacket or handbag, Sharon,' the instructor explained. 'We don't want to take anything on the plane that adds extra weight. These planes are so small that even those things will affect the plane's ability to fly effectively.'

We went through the pre-flight checks, and finally, we were taxiing out to the runway. I used to think that the Dash 8s, those commuter planes that do the runs between capital cities, were small until I came nose to nose with one in my little training plane. They are huge, absolutely huge, compared to a little Cessna!

You may have heard that a fear of flying disappears once you are flying the plane yourself because you feel more in control. I found that was complete rubbish. The more I learnt, the more I realized I did not know. I was definitely safer under the stewardship of a Qantas pilot than I was in charge of this little flying machine.

My training plane had the registration number WWS, so therefore its call sign was *Whisky, Whisky, Sierra.* I'm an alcoholic, so there's some irony in that, isn't there? That used to make me smile every time I called the air control tower.

Determined to one day fly this plane solo, I turned up religiously for my lessons twice a week. I don't want you to think that my fear of flying went away any time soon. Every morning, I would wake up in the hope that the instructor would call me to say it was too windy to fly that day, or that he was sick, or even that aliens were coming down—I was just hoping I wouldn't have to fly that day. But the important thing was that I *never* cancelled a flying lesson myself. Every single time, I turned up to fly, full of fear, and I did it anyway.

I don't remember when my fear of flying went away, but it was sometime after I did the enforced incipient spins (where you head the plane nose-down towards the ground, spin three times, and then pull the plane back to safety) and sometime before the practice crash landings.

It takes a minimum of twenty hours of flying time before they allow you to fly alone. I don't pretend that I was good at this or anything, because after thirty-five hours, they finally said I was able to fly the plane solo.

They don't tend to give you any notice that they are going to let you fly solo. I believe it is so that you do not have a chance to get too scared. Good idea.

Once you are up there, though, all on your own, you only have two choices:

    a)   Remember everything they told you and land the damn plane.
    b)   Crash.

I decided to go with plan A.

Once I flew that plane solo, I knew that my 'fear' lesson was learned. The lesson I had learned was that *fear itself would not kill me*. This in itself is a huge lesson and can be quite life-changing for anyone who cares to learn it. So, for me, this was a huge turning point because I had learnt that I could be afraid of something physical and it would not actually kill me to be afraid. This meant I was able to face my emotional fears and know that they too would not kill me. Emotional fears for me included fear of rejection, fear of people not liking me, fear of not being successful, and fear of not being good enough, but above all, fear of not being loved.

These fears were holding me back so much that I was not being my *best self.* I was spending so much of my emotional energy worrying about these things that I was not spending my time living my best life. So, little by little (and I mean two steps forward, one step back), I started dealing with my emotional fears.

The turnaround point for me came when my self-esteem started to improve. I started to realize that there is no point being fearful of what people think of me because I am what I am, and I have no control over what they think of me. I was spending so much time being fearful about being good enough that I was not being the best I could be. I have found that there are a lot of paradoxes in life, many of which became apparent during my recovery. This is a clear paradox showing that the more you let go of your fear, the less fearful you become.

The interesting thing was that until now, I had thought I was *so* special. I thought I was the only one who felt like this.

What I did not realize at the time is that a lot of people live in fear to some extent or another. These people, normal people, are still fearful sometimes, and they just allow themselves to feel the fear and then they just *resume without fuss.*

A basic level of fear for survival is healthy. It is what has kept us alive for hundreds of thousands of years. But this is all we need, *a basic level of fear.*

All other fear will lead to a smaller life.

We need to trust ourselves a bit more. A friend of mine is afraid of snakes. He has two choices as to how to handle this fear. He can keep it as a healthy fear (as we all should, because some snakes can in fact kill you), or he can let it rule his life.

An unhealthy way for him to respond to his fear would be if he were never to go anywhere where there could be a snake. So he would make his life smaller by never going to a zoo, park, river, lake, bush, or friend who lives in the country.

A healthy way for him to respond to this fear is for him to feel his fear and then make *informed decisions* on what is reasonably safe to do. So, it would not be safe for him to walk through the bush in thongs on a hot summer day when snakes are at their fastest. However, if he trusts himself and makes a logical and sensible choice, he will still go and visit his friend in the country and walk in reasonably safe areas with reasonably sensible shoes. We need to trust ourselves and not let the fear take control.

Fear is another of those feelings that we spend our whole lives trying to avoid, when instead we need to change the way we feel about fear. Just feel the fear, and let it go.

I have one other important belief about fear. Fear is quite an immature feeling, as it means that you still believe you have the ultimate control to stop *anything* bad happening to you. You don't. The universe, or whichever god you choose to believe in, has the final decision on that, and you cannot control it. Much of our fear is based on the immature idea that we have total control.

Ultimately, my final rock bottom and then admission into detox were really all the information I needed to learn that I did not have control over everything I feared, and that fear was pointless. Not being good enough, people finding out about my drinking, not being able to work hard enough, not being a good enough mother—these were all the things I feared the most. And all these things happened to me the day I hit rock bottom, and so you see, being overly fearful made everything I feared actually happen.

And so I moved forward in my still-early sobriety with the knowledge that fear is part of my life and is not to be avoided, but just felt.

Remember, life is not measured by the number of breaths you take; it is measured by the moments that take your breath away.

Charm 3:

Fear itself will not kill you.

Chapter 4

The Prison in Our Minds

(Tolerance)

There are no extra pieces in the universe. Everyone is here because she has a place to fill, and every piece must fit itself into the big jigsaw puzzle.
—Deepak Chopra

One year to the day since my first sober day, I was asked if I would consider being part of a mentoring program in the new prison that was due to open in Canberra.

I was quite honored to be considered for this, as I felt that maybe that meant I knew something about recovery. This kind of surprised me, since some days I woke up (and still do) thinking I still had so much to learn.

I'm not sure about you, but I had never been into a prison and had no idea of what to expect.

The first step was to do the security training that was required before I was approved to enter the prison. I found the course quite interesting. We learnt a lot about prison culture and prison currency, and I didn't even know there was such a thing. They showed us actual footage of prison inmates being killed in Australian prisons so that we could see how quickly violence could escalate between the inmates. I discovered that I must watch too much *Law and Order,* because I was not nearly as shocked as I maybe should have been at the violence. Not everyone decided to go through with volunteering at the prison, but I felt there was something to learn.

After I had received my security clearance, I had an iris scan done because that is one of the security measures used in the new prison. It was very *Charlie's Angels* and 007, and I must say that I enjoyed all the fun of this new technology.

Going into the prison is similar to going through airport security, with the iris scan checks added in a couple of times for good measure. You are not allowed to take anything into the prison in case it is turned into a weapon. Not even something as simple as a pen, and definitely not a mobile phone. I felt completely naked without my mobile phone. When was the last time you went into what could be a dangerous situation without your phone?

On my first visit to the prison, I was *nervous*. I was afraid that I would have nothing to offer these women. What on earth could a mother from the suburbs have to offer these hardened criminals?

It was very confronting to go into a situation where I was the odd one out. It reminded me very much of being the new kid at school, the out-of-place one with the wrong uniform on.

Walking into the prison for the first time was like walking into a bad 1970s school camp, which was pretty amazing, since it was only a week old. I guess they had to construct this thing on a pretty tight budget, so aesthetics were not high on their list. There were no white jumpsuits with black arrows here and not even any orange overalls (I think I *do* watch too much American TV), but the clothing, and everything else, is still all about the function in prison, not the fashion.

Each fortnight as I was led through security into the women's section, the guards would ask around the 'houses' (new age name for cells) and see if anyone wanted to come up and have a chat.

The women in the prison ranged in age from early adulthood right through to grandmas. I would chat to women from all of these age ranges. Many of the women did not get very many visitors, often not wanting to tell their young children that they were in gaol. Similar to an alcoholic's story, these ladies' journeys had spiraled downwards, and they had left a trail of destruction to the relationships of the people who cared for them.

And with that, I started to see the similarities in our lives.

One afternoon, I had been led into the women's section of the prison, and I sat waiting in one of the small meeting rooms where we would sit. We would not sit in the open visitors' areas, as these are quite communal, without privacy, and everyone can hear what you are saying. The rooms we went to were more like very small conference rooms. I always guessed these were the rooms where the women would meet their legal representation and welfare officers and the like. One side of each conference room was glass, so the guards could see each room from their central station. As I sat and waited that day, a couple of ladies at a time wandered in over a period of ten or so minutes, until everyone was there who wanted to come. We had a small group of about six women and me. As the ladies began to talk that day, they spoke a lot about their time before they had come to prison. About their marriages and their extended families and their children. So much of what these women said that day was exactly—I'm talking word for word—what I had been saying not one year earlier, before I started my recovery journey.

These women, just like me, struggled with the need to over-function and overprotect the ones they loved, which left the women without the ability for self-care. At least their journey into the prison was teaching them self-protection as a first step to self-care.

The discussion centred around not what these women could do for themselves, but for their loved ones on the outside, and what these women could do to assist emotionally with some situation going on in their loved ones' lives.

At first, I was astounded that these women should so clearly be focusing on changes they should make in their own lives, and instead they were worried about other people. They were managing their anxieties and fears for themselves through their codependency with others.

The similarity to me, in the midst of my active alcoholism, was clear. I too had managed my anxieties and fears in my life through over-functioning and over-caring for the people I loved, when in fact I should have been focusing on my own self-care. My alcoholism should have been my primary area of concern before I was able to be any kind of support to the people I loved.

In these women, I could see my own journey. Even though I had initially thought our lives were so different, in fact we were all very, very similar.

A quote that would often come to mind as I would leave the prison was 'There but for the grace of God go I.' Meaning, but for a few small tweaks in the way my life had gone, this too could have been me.

I had found the same situation when I had first started attending recovery groups for alcoholism. These groups often had mostly men in attendance, and mostly much older than me, and mostly with much different life stories from mine. In the beginning, I had not met an alcoholic mum from the suburbs amongst these people, and I did not see how their experiences could help me with mine at all.

In my desperation, I sat and listened to what these men were saying about their journeys, both during their active drinking careers and also their recovery. To my amazement, when they talked, it was like they were telling my story. The pain they had gone through, the people in their lives they had affected, their despair at ever being able to stop drinking.

My time in these recovery groups and with the women in the prison taught me that no matter how different we all look on the outside, we are all very similar on the inside.

I think of everyone in the world being like a gift, wrapped up in layers and layers of wrapping paper. Each layer of paper is a different colour and texture. As we go through our journey, we peel off the layers of gift-wrapping to discover another layer underneath. Along your journey, you may find other people who are up to the same layer as you, so they will look and feel the same colour and texture as you. It will be easier to see their point of view and understand them because they look the same as you on the outside. Then there will be other people who will be up to a different layer from you, and so they will look and feel different. It will be harder to see their point of view and situation because they look different from you, but underneath it all, we are all the same gift.

This is why it is important to remember that everyone is at a different place in their journeys in this life. They may look different and sound different at the moment, and they may even think differently from you because they are at different places in their lives from you. It does not make them wrong; it just makes them different. Underneath it all, they will have a lot of similarities to you.

Learn to look through what people initially show you on the outside to see their life's work underneath the gift-wrapping. Look at the resemblances between yourself and all of the other people around you so that you may be blessed enough to see who they really are.

Life is only interesting because every person in the world has something different to offer, and *normal is just a cycle on the washing machine.*

These women, even in their own prison of pain and torment, taught me that every person I meet on my journey has something to teach me. I just need to be open to seeing who they really are.

Charm 4:

*Look for the similarities in others
not the differences.*

Chapter 5

The Leaky Bucket of Water

(Emotional Growth)

You did what you knew how to do, and then when you knew better, you did better.
—Maya Angelou

By now, I was one year into my journey of recovery, and our lives were tracking along, looking from the outside like everything was going well. Simon was running the business, and Josie and Jackson were going along well at school. Now that I was sober, I could actually do *even more* than I was doing when I was drinking, so I was over-functioning for the family and the house (and anyone else who would let me). The house was beautiful. I hosted parties, we attended parties, and most of our friends, who had also not wanted to talk about the 'elephant in the room', went along as if nothing had happened. My sobriety was never discussed with the majority of people we knew. We all looked happy and healthy, like that bump in our otherwise perfect life had been ironed out.

I no longer had that all-encompassing ache to pick up a drink. My body had lost the urgent need for the alcohol itself, but I still didn't have the emotional capacity to cope with life. That meant that I was still in a fair amount of emotional pain most of the time. But no one outside of our family would have known this.

During this first year of my sobriety, I had met a wise, long-time sober alcoholic, Anne. Anne lived in Sydney but visited Canberra often enough for me to see her regularly. Anne had already helped me considerably in dealing with the early stages of my recovery. She had helped me to deal with my feelings that at that time I did not understand, and she had helped me understand the importance of living with my fears and resuming my life without fuss.

One morning, around this time of my first sobriety birthday, Anne and I met for a coffee, and we were talking a lot about the pain I still lived with every day. I remember saying to her, 'Anne, I don't understand how I can be in this much pain when I am trying so hard to make everything right for everyone.'

She replied, 'Sharon, I know you love your kids and your husband, but you need to remember that your recovery must come before everything else. You need to learn the value of your own self-care.

You can only help others when you have helped yourself. If you do not learn how to deal with the pain you are in, you will eventually pick up a drink.'

I remember quite clearly that as Anne was saying this to me, I was nodding my head so that she would think I was agreeing with her—but inside my mind, I was shaking my head, because there was just no way I could comprehend any kind of self-care.

What I could comprehend, though, was that if I learnt a lesson, like the ones I had already learnt about feelings and fear, then the pain in those areas would start to dissipate. I spoke to Anne about learning some more lessons so that the pain would start to go away. She said, 'Sharon, this is emotional growth, and it is the key to everything.'

So, as I went on my journey of emotional growth, I learnt one thing for sure: *Insanity is the act of repeating the same behaviours and expecting a different outcome.*

It is a mystery to me, but true all the same, that humans do seem less likely to make changes for emotional pain than they are for physical pain.

For example, if you were to stick your hand on the hot plate and burn your hand, you would learn that putting your hand on the hot stove hurt, and therefore you would not do it again. You would probably only need to do this once to learn this lesson.

How often have you seen a friend go out with someone who treats her badly and then hurts her, and she either goes back to the same guy or goes out with the same *type* of guy again?

Unlike the stove incident, which only took us once to learn, the man incident seems to take us quite a lot more pain before we start learning *not* to repeat that behaviour.

As we grow from teenagers into young adults, we do not have the emotional tools to deal with all the things that life has thrown at us. We have two choices: we can learn from what happens to us and respond to situations in a different way so that they don't hurt so much, or alternatively, we can *not* learn from those experiences—we can continue to react and respond in the same ways as we always do. As I have mentioned, this type of behaviour is insane because we are expecting a different outcome.

For me, like a lot of people who quit drinking, I thought that when I stopped drinking, all my other problems would go away.

At that time, I knew I was desperately unhappy, but of course I thought it was all related to my drinking. I did not even know the level of unresolved issues I had sitting in my past. As I see it, each time I had an issue during my life, whether it was a big one or a small one, I had drunk through it instead of feeling the feelings and growing through the experience. It never occurred to me during my early adulthood that I was avoiding the lessons from all my life experiences by drinking through them, and therefore I was not allowing myself to grow.

I remember, a few years before the end of my drinking, a friend of mine called me to tell me that she was separating from her husband. 'Great,' was my response. 'Let's go out and commiserate,' I said, with the idea of drinking large amounts of alcohol so she could wipe herself out and forget about it (because that is what I would have done).

As she was not a big drinker—and more importantly, she obviously had more emotional maturity than I—her next words were an absolute mystery to me.

'No, Sharon, I need to be completely *present* right now and allow myself to feel these feelings and start the grieving process of my divorce, so no, drinking won't help that at all.'

I thought this was madness. The thought of 'feeling feelings' and 'going through a process' was so foreign to me. I thought the whole idea of life was to firstly do everything you could to avoid feelings and then, if you were unfortunate enough to have a feeling, to get rid of it as quickly as possible. I was very confused as to why my friend would want to *feel* her *feelings*. I had no idea that this was what led to emotional growth.

I can see now that emotional growth is the only way of stopping those destructive behaviours that cause us so much pain. Remember that we cannot change the things around us; we can only change the way we respond to them. Emotional growth is the best way to learn how to respond better to each and every situation that life continues to throw at us.

Now, many people have big things happen in their lives that make them have that 'light bulb' moment when they realize they must make changes. In recovery from addiction, this is often called a rock bottom.

My rock bottom was fabulous, as far as rock bottoms go. I nearly died. Can't get much rockier than that. Of course, now I am very grateful that my rock bottom was so dramatic because, as I see it, it did not give me any choice but to work out what the hell was wrong with my life and do something about it.

But most people who are not in the grips of such a horrific addiction as mine are not so lucky as to hit a hard rock bottom, as I did. So they will drag themselves along that bottom for years and sometimes forever, and I understand that this can be very painful.

When I first stopped drinking, I did not know that I still had a whole journey ahead of me. When I quit drinking, all I did was clear my head long enough to now start the journey of emotional growth. It would take years to even begin to catch up on all the lost years of my drinking career.

An important point to remember is that it does not have to be an addiction to force emotional growth upon you. I recently saw Olivia Newton-John interviewed by Andrew Denton. She was talking about when she got diagnosed with cancer. When she told a close friend of hers, who is a Buddhist, that she had cancer, he had said, 'Congratulations, now you will grow.' She said that at the time, she had no idea what he was talking about, but now that she is on a journey of emotional growth, kick-started by her cancer diagnosis, she understands the benefits of growth.

As far as emotional growth goes, I found that the issues that keep arising are probably the ones you need to do some work on. Remember, you cannot change the other people, places, or things; you can only change the way you respond to them. So your lesson is to learn how to deal better with these situations, and you will find they hurt less and less every time.

I found that sometimes a particular lesson or issue was just too painful for me to deal with at that stage of my journey. I personally find that I get hurt the most when I am dealing with issues related to the people I love the most. I think this is because it is with these people that I have the most to lose.

After my insightful discussion with Anne that day about emotional growth, I then made it my job in recovery to work on my emotional growth as much as I could. I would look for situations everywhere that would be growth opportunities for me. At one point, though, I forgot that emotional growth is a life-long journey and there was no deadline for me to get this finished. I have had times when I have had to put a particular issue on hold until I was emotionally ready to deal with it.

This happened to me on the Christmas not long after my first sobriety birthday. We had just come back from our holiday to the UK (I use the term *holiday* loosely because twenty-four/seven arrangements for an over-functioning codependent on holiday are enormously stressful); we had end-of-year functions and events for family, the business, and the school community; and we had some life-threatening illnesses in some extended family members.

I was over-managing all of these situations. Not surprisingly, I ended up struggling emotionally during this time and ended up in my therapist's office early one Monday morning over what was, essentially, a relatively minor matter with my daughter.

The therapist gave me the following analogy: She said that we could think of our emotions like the water level filling up in a bucket. Each day, drips of emotional water go into the bucket, and we can cope with that till it is pretty much full. Every now and again, we get a bigger issue that is like a cupful of water, and it fills the bucket quicker. Now, if we are looking after our emotional health, we will make sure that if the bucket gets too full, we have the mechanism to pull out the plug from the bottom of the emotional bucket and empty some of the water. We can do this best by making sure we have enough quality time for emotional growth. For example, we could meditate, go to church, talk to a friend, see a therapist or counselor, or just practice some mindfulness. By doing any of these things, we will empty the emotional bucket enough for it to cope with some more.

Well, as an alcoholic in recovery, still unable to deal with all my emotions, my bucket was *full, full, full.* So the one little issue that came up between my daughter and myself was blown up out of proportion and became quite painful for everyone involved.

So at that time, I had to put that growth area on hold until my bucket was a little emptier and then I was able to work on those things with my daughter at a later time.

However, whenever my emotional bucket has got some room in it, I jump at the chance to pour some more water in it and get a bit of emotional growth.

I try to use every experience to feel those all-important feelings and learn something. I find that the key to emotional growth is *not* to repeat old behaviours and expect something different to happen, and also *not to try to be right all the time*. If we are right all the time, then we cannot possibly learn anything. I also try to remember that we do not need to lay blame with anyone; we just need to work out how to do it better next time.

Now, most lessons are learnt a little bit at a time and with lots of practice. Not many of us are lucky enough to have a light bulb moment and suddenly understand this lesson and all its implications. And sometimes, even if we do have some kind of epiphany, we are so used to the old behaviour that it actually takes a while to change the old ways to the new.

What I have learnt is that by working on our emotional growth, we are creating a nice plughole in the emotional bucket so that water can drain gradually out and so that we do not overflow so often.

The important lesson about emotional growth is to know that, as with so many things, you do not have control over the things that happen around you—but you do have the choice to head on a journey of emotional growth any time you would like. You do not need to wait until you are in unbearable amounts of pain, and you do not need to wait until you hit any kind of rock bottom.

So as I moved through this second year of my recovery, I learned that life is change and growth is optional. With Anne as my guide, I chose wisely and chose to continue my journey with emotional growth.

Charm 5:

*The journey of emotional growth
will be painful at times, but no one
who has undertaken it has regretted
that they began.*

Chapter 6

Be the Solution

(Addiction)

Health is what all my friends are drinking to before they fall down.

—Phyllis Diller

It was at this time, as I was moving through my second year of sobriety, that I started to notice how many women, not only alcoholics, seemed to be suffering some of the same pain that I was. It seemed that some women would realise that I was on some kind of journey and it would open dialogue between us about their own hurt. I saw that some women managed their pain with addiction, but I discovered that there are many ways that we manage our pain and anxiety.

So before you turn the page to skip this chapter because it does not apply to you, just read on for a little while, as I think there is still a lesson here for everyone.

First, I would like to speak to those amongst you who know that you have a problem and don't think you can do anything about it. I was just like you.

I used to read self-help books to try to work out what was wrong with me. When they came to the chapter on addiction, it would usually say, 'There is nothing you can do until you go and see a professional and stop drinking/drugging/eating, and then you can work on yourself.' I would read those bits and think, *That's okay for them to say, but I'm not ready to stop drinking, and I can't live without it,* or *I don't need to stop drinking. I can fix everything else and I won't need to stop drinking.*

Wrong.

An addicted mind can, and does, convince itself of anything at all in order to avoid dealing with its addiction. *Anything.*

If you are addicted to something, then you have two choices:

1. Work on your addiction recovery, OR
2. Spiral downhill to death and/or devastation.

That's it. And don't think you are different from everyone else, because you are not.

There are no other choices. There is no quick fix, no pill, no middle road, and absolutely no easy way.

So if you are not working on your addiction in recovery, then by definition you are choosing the path to your own destruction.

Going into recovery, and dedicating yourself to it, will be the single hardest thing you have ever done in your life.

You will have to go to levels of emotional pain that you did not even know existed. You will have to face every single thing you have been spending your whole life avoiding. You will have to turn over every rock, go down every hole, and drag your sad, remorseful soul through all the stuff that you and your addiction left behind.

And if you do these things, then I can promise you this: Even your worst day in recovery will be better than any day you have had in the depth of your addiction.

So, what is an addiction?

Over the years, I have read many definitions of addiction, but I think the most understandable definition is this: *Overuse of a substance or activity becomes an addiction when the negative outcomes attached to that behaviour are diminished or ignored.*

In other words, if you ignore it when the negatives attached to your behaviours clearly outweigh the positives, then you are an addict.

Remember addiction can come in many forms, and can range from addictions to alcohol, drugs, food and nicotine right through to addictions to sex, gambling, spending, exercise and work; and this is to just to name a few!

As for me, I had never actually told myself that I was an alcoholic, and until that day in the hospital when I was near death, no one had ever told me that either.

Although I had known for a long time that I could not stop my drinking, I had not labeled it as alcoholism. I thought the definition of an alcoholic was an old homeless guy who drank his grog from a bottle in a brown paper bag on a bench in the park.

So, it is very ironic to think that towards the end of my drinking, when I was unable to drive anymore, I would walk my kids to school in the mornings—still drunk, of course, as by this time, I was drinking all the time, even when I woke up in the morning. I would pull on my sneakers, fill up my drink bottle with more grog, and walk the kids to school.

One morning towards the end, I was able to get the kids down to school, but by that time, I had polished off nearly a full drink bottle of grog along the way, and I was not in any fit state to walk back home again. I made it across the road from school and fell asleep on the bench near the bus stop and continued to drink from the bottle of grog in hand.

So I thought an alcoholic was someone who slept on a park bench and drank their alcohol from a disguised drinking bottle. I *was* someone who was asleep on a bench drinking alcohol from a disguised drinking bottle.

I was a drunk.

My alcoholic mind, in its absolute obsession with preventing me from admitting my alcoholism, did not see this at all.

I will share with you a very important point about addicts. This information is important if it is you who is the addict or if you care for someone who is an addict.

In my experience, an addict *will not*, I repeat, *will not*, get long-term, good quality recovery unless they have hit their own *rock bottom*.

So what is a rock bottom?

The answer is that everybody's rock bottom is different. I feel very blessed every day that my rock bottom was very near death. So for me I know that if I ever, ever pick up a drink again, then it is as simple as this: *To drink is to die.* My rock bottom is very clear and very definable. Not everyone is 'blessed' this way. If their rock bottom is not so clear-cut, then it is sometimes a bit easier to forget and therefore can be easier to relapse.

For some people, their rock bottom can be losing their license through drunk driving. For some people, it can be the end of a marriage. For some people, it can be losing their kids. I have heard of people who have killed people during an alcoholic blackout and that is still not enough of a rock bottom for them to stop drinking.

My message from this is that it does not matter how much you care about an addict; you cannot *make addicts* stop their addiction. *You can't.* You must let addicts decide for themselves when they have hit their rock bottom, and you must allow them to go into recovery when they are able.

However, by the same token, you must not *enable* the addict either. You must look after yourself and seek help for yourself. Learn about self-care, letting go of control, establishing healthy boundaries, and sticking to them.

Now I would like to talk for a minute to those people among us who may not yet be classified as addicts, as the activity or substance is not yet adversely affecting their lives, but it may be something they do to excess and you wonder why.

The simple answer is that routine and repetition are at the core of our most basic animal instinct to manage anxiety. Nothing calms us like the familiar.

I believe that we make the majority of our decisions—both big and small—based on fear. I believe that unless we actively choose to live otherwise, our most basic instinct is to avoid feeling fear.

So our most basic behaviour is to live in fear, and our most basic response is to enable repetitive behaviours to make us feel less fearful or anxious. That is how we survive.

And that's where addiction comes in. As I have mentioned, addiction can come in many forms and for many reasons. Alcoholism itself is interesting as far as addictions go. I believe in the 'disease' concept of alcoholism, which means that those of us who are alcoholics are born with it, and it cannot be cured. It is a genetic defect that leaves our bodies needing alcohol with the same necessity as water, food, and air. This means that I was on a steady decline from the minute I picked up a drink, and my only prevention from active alcoholism is abstinence. That means I can never pick up a drink again as long as I live. I think of alcoholism as being like being born with type 1 diabetes. Being born with diabetes is not the fault of the diabetic; but if you continually come home to find that your loved one who is diabetic has eaten sugar again and is on the floor in a near-coma, eventually you need that person to take responsibility for the illness (even though it was not his or her fault) by ceasing to eat sugar. I believe the same goes for alcoholics. If they drink when they know they can't and they are on the floor in a near-coma again, you will eventually need *them* to take responsibility for their illness and cease their alcohol consumption.

I found that whatever the reason for my alcoholism, my overuse of alcohol left me with an inability to deal with even the most basic level of anxiety. My alcohol consumption soon became my tool to handle all my feelings, good and bad, which in the end left me unable to feel and deal with feeling at all. So, like all addicts, I am a prime candidate for some type of cross-addiction as we try to swap one form of repetitive behaviour for another in an attempt to relieve our anxieties. The only solution to this is some form of emotional growth. I am grateful that I learnt this lesson quickly before I relieved my anxieties with some other addiction.

If addiction becomes part of your life, it becomes a prison that cannot be escaped easily. It is relentless and chronic. If you have an addiction, start your journey now with one small step forward by asking for help.

Almost everyone is touched by addiction in themselves or someone they know or love. It is an epidemic of mammoth proportions which can best be dealt with by learning healthy anxiety management tools for you and your loved ones.

So if you know or love someone who is addicted, the best advice I can give you is to work on your own self-care. Get started today. Learn about your boundaries and recognize that you *cannot* fix the other person. If you think you have behaviour that is addictive, or becoming addictive, do something about it. It can, and will, only spiral downhill until you start to deal with it. Dealing with addictions is learning how to manage anxiety. You cannot begin your journey towards a happier life until you have done that.

Living with an addiction, or an addict, is like living in chains. Free yourself from the prison of your addiction or your need to help the addict. If you have a hole in your heart shaped like addiction, you need to learn to fill that hole with joy that you will find in this journey.

Charm 6:

The *journey of recovery out of* *addiction must be* undertaken willingly by the addict, *not by the addict's loved ones.*

Chapter 7

Blonde Streaks and Light Bulbs

(Truth)

There are things known, and things that are
unknown, and in between is perception.
—Aldous Huxley

My next lesson came to me not long after Christmas during my second year, and it was the lesson on truth. The interesting thing is that I *thought* I knew about truth already. I thought I knew what truth was, because I thought everyone's version of truth was the same as mine.

You see, when I was drinking and I did not have the emotional maturity to look at things differently, I thought truth was very simple.

I thought there were truth and lies, right and wrong, black and white. No grey.

So that realization that there could be different versions of what the truth was became very apparent to me one day after Christmas that year, at the end of school holidays.

I had made an appointment for my children at the hairdresser's to have their hair cut and have blonde tips put through their hair. I had been having blonde tips put through their hair since they were about six years old. The reason for this went as far back as any of my misguided reasons for doing anything at that time.

When I was growing up poor, we certainly did not have money to have things like blonde tips put in our hair. I remember when I would look longingly at all the popular kids in each of the schools I went to as their beautifully golden streaks shone their way blissfully through the struggles of teenage life in the 80s.

So of course, I had a strong idea that blonde streaks equals money which equals happiness. Therefore, as an adult, from the day I could afford it, I had blonde streaks in my hair, and therefore, as soon as I could reasonably get a hairdresser to do it, I got the same done with the kids.

It never, ever occurred to me that they would not want to have blonde streaks. To me, that would be like . . . well, actually, I don't know what that would be like because that was *my truth*.

So on this day, I had this simple, yet immediate moment when I realized that not everyone's truth was the same as mine, least of all my children's.

I was waiting for the kids to finish getting ready so I could drive them to the hairdresser when Josie said simply, quietly, and without anger or resentment, 'Mum, I don't think I want to get blonde streaks anymore.'

Boom! Light bulb moment.

Until that moment, it had never occurred to me that everyone in the world did not want blonde streaks. Right then, for the first time, it occurred to me that there were other people who could afford blonde streaks and apparently chose not to have them. What a revelation.

This light bulb moment opened up a whole new thought process for me and allowed me to realize that there were lots and lots of things that people could in fact have different opinions on, otherwise known as their truths, and neither was right or wrong, just different.

I spoke to Anne about this at one of our regular get-togethers. She explained to me that the next important thing to learn about other people's truths was that if a person had a different truth from mine, it was actually not my job to change the other person's mind to align with my truth. Wow! This was a great realization for me, and a great relief. Not everyone in the world does, or needs to, have the same truths and values as I do, and I can stop wasting my time trying to convince them how right my truth is.

Most often, trying to convince other people of a different truth from their own before they are ready to hear it will only end in disagreement and argument.

Everybody's version of the truth may be different, and correct, but the most important thing to remember is that even if you do disagree with someone on their version of the truth, *would you rather be right or happy?*

The best story I have ever heard to explain this is 'The Wise Men and the Elephant', which, I understand, was originally an Indian fable. It is translated something like this:

There were six wise men that were all blind. The group of men had been told about an animal called an elephant, but none of them had seen one, and they asked a seeing man to tell them what it looked like. His reply was, 'You can go in and feel him for yourself, and then you will know what he looks like.'

So each of the six men entered the room with the elephant.

The first man went in, and the first thing he came to was the elephant's tusk. He felt the tusk, turned, and left the room happy that he knew what an elephant looked like.

The second man went into the room with the elephant, and the first thing he touched was the trunk. He too was satisfied that he now knew what an elephant looked like.

This continued on as the third felt the ear, the fourth felt a foot, the fifth ran into the elephant's enormous back, and finally, the sixth felt the tail.

Once they had all finished, the sighted man asked, 'Are you happy now that you know what an elephant looks like?'

'Yes,' the first man, who had touched the tusk, called out. 'The elephant is sharp like a spear.'

The second, who had touched the trunk, shouted, 'No, no, what are you talking about? The elephant is just like a snake.'

The third, who had felt the ear, added, 'No, no, you are both wrong. The elephant is a fan to cool us when we are hot.'

This carried on as the fourth, fifth, and sixth men piped in with their ideas of what the elephant looked like.

They all screamed and shouted as they tried to get the other blind men in the group to see *their truth*.

Of course, the moral to this story is that in fact people may see the truth differently, but it does not necessarily make you right and them wrong, or vice versa.

I used this initial light bulb moment on truth as the kick-start to understanding so much more about how each person's truth affects his or her choices and decisions every single day. Each person's version of the truth is clearly coloured by his or her experiences, upbringing, and outlook on life.

It is important to know, and to keep, your own truths important to you. However, it is just as important to remember that another person's truth can be different from yours. My daughter knows that her comment that day at the hairdresser was a light bulb moment for me. Since then, we have discussed it numerous times as I have pondered its influence on my life. Recently in one of those discussions, she put it most eloquently when she said, 'It is just as important to value another person's truth as it is to know your own.'

Charm 7:

Truth is relative, not an absolute.

Chapter 8

Live Like a Dog

(Happiness)

We tend to forget that happiness doesn't come as a result of getting something we don't have, but rather of recognizing and appreciating what we do have.

—*Frederick Koenig*

As I tracked on forward through my second year of sobriety, I was becoming more and more disillusioned about finding happiness. All of my life, I had believed that happiness would come to me when I had everything I wanted. I believed that everything I wanted was to be married and stay married, no matter what, and also to have happy, healthy kids and of course, to have lots of money.

I have met a lot of women who think that. I have met women right through the spectrum of society, from women in prison (drug money) right through to the wives of multimillionaire businessmen. Many of them believed that these things would make them happy, and they too are surprised that they are not happy when they do get these things.

Many of these women gave me the reasons why they were unhappy. I would like to say that they were wide and varied, *but* they were not. Every single one of those women told me that she too had thought money and marriage would bring her happiness. And it had not. I found admitting that I was not happy was one of the hardest emotional things to do because it felt like everything I had worked for, the plan I had had, all the years of work until now, were wasted. I think that is why a lot of women are not willing to admit they are not happy, and so we work a little harder.

I had an important turning point one day in my journey towards happiness when I was once again up late at night cleaning, organizing, packing, and arranging for the well-being of the lives of the three people I cared the most for. The kids were safely tucked up in bed, and Simon was out in the shed enjoying his car restoration activities that brought him happiness.

I was exhausted. I had been up since 4:30 a.m. I had been working all day, and I still had a list as long as your arm. I really needed to be in bed. Simon came out from the shed and asked me something minor about the details of an event being held the next day. I was left feeling like he wanted me to do even more for the function. Well,

I flipped out with words full of anger, resentment, exhaustion, and complete frustration! How the hell could I do any more than I was doing to keep everyone happy, let alone be happy myself?

I slumped down onto the lounge and cried the tears of the exhausted. Deep, howling tears of a soul with nothing left to give. That was it—I had nothing left to give. Right then, at that moment, I realized I could not find my own happiness by making other people happy. I knew right then that I could not find it in other people or in other things. I needed to find my own happiness, and I was the only one responsible for that and the only one to blame for not having found it yet. And I was sick of waiting! I was going to work out how to be happy, and I was going to do it now.

I started doing a lot of reading about happiness, and I spoke to people who I believed might actually be happy. Some of these people were people whom just years before, I would have dismissed because they did not have the things that I thought would bring happiness. These people had found happiness without things. Some of these people had even learnt how to be happy in adverse conditions. It was not like they were all sitting around counting their millions or anything; they were just *happy*.

So, while I read and talked to people about happiness, I found that it is a very empowering emotion because only I have the power to make me happy, and only I have the power to take it away. It is a choice to be happy. And in fact, if you wait until you have everything that you think will make you happy, you will never be happy.

So you do not wait to find it; you must *find it now* if you ever want to get it.

Here are some of the reasons I have heard as to why people cannot be happy. They are waiting for the right boyfriend, their first job, their first car, the engagement, the wedding, or their first house. Then, they are waiting for that pay rise and then for their first baby.

Next, they are waiting for a boy instead of the girl, and of course for the time when they lose the baby fat. Then for when the kids go to school, and then for when they've paid off the house, and then for when they can finally afford the holiday house. Then for a second car and then for the new business to take off. Then for the kids to finish school, for the holiday house to be paid off, and then for enough money to retire. And then, guess what? They're dead.

Maybe by this time, you will finally be happy because you finally have everything you wanted. Or maybe you won't because you have never learnt how to be happy along the way.

Now, here is a completely different way to think about it.

Think like a dog!

Have you ever noticed this about a dog? He is sound asleep when you get home. As soon as he sees you, he jumps up, his tail starts wagging, and he runs over to you with excitement.

Wow! he is thinking. *There's my owner. That's my* favourite *thing!* He's happy!

Then five minutes later, he is back on the lounge when you reach into the cupboard, grab the dog food, and call to your little doggie as you walk towards his bowl. He jumps up off the lounge, tail wagging again, and runs towards the bowl.

Wow! he thinks again. *Food! That's my* favourite *thing!* He's happy!

While he is eating his dinner, you wander inside and get changed into your comfy after-work clothes. You walk back outside to see how the dog is going with his dinner. You notice his favourite chew toy in the yard as you carefully tread onto the grass. You pick up the chew toy and throw it enthusiastically in the dog's direction.

Wow! he thinks to himself with surprise. *Chew-toy, that's my favourite thing!* As he lifts his head, his tail starts wagging again, and he leaps upward towards the toy.

Unfortunately, just then the hard corner of the chew toy hits the dog's head just above his eye as he enthusiastically tries to grab the toy.

The dog yelps in pain. His tail stops wagging, and he stands still for a second or two as he contemplates the pain near his eye.

'Oh, lovely boy,' you say in a soft, kind voice as you walk towards him with your outstretched hand. 'Are you okay? That bad old toy hit you right on the head . . .'

Wow! he thinks as he lifts his head again and sees you coming towards him. *There's my owner. That's my* favourite *thing!* He's happy again!

Isn't that just the kind of behaviour you see from your dog every day? Can you see the lesson that the dog can teach us here?

The secret is that the dog *lives in the moment.*

The dog enjoys each moment of happiness as it is handed to him. He is not thinking whether the last moment was better than this one, or how good the next one will be. He only thinks about what is going on right now and how good it is.

Now, of course you are thinking that not every moment in your life is good, so how can you be happy all the time? That's true; you can't. But did you see what the dog did when the toy hit him in the head? He felt the pain and accepted it, and then when he was able, he moved on. He didn't think about it once the pain was bearable; instead, he jumped up at the next great opportunity (being his owner giving him a nice pat) once it came to him. *Remember that one bad thing happening in a day does not make it a bad day.*

I know that people new to this concept will think it is much too simplistic and that there must be a much more complicated theory to happiness. You can read every book that was ever written about happiness (and of course I suggest you do, as they are much more eloquent than me), but they all come down to this one key point.

Live in the moment.

'Stuff' will not make you happier. People will not make you happier. There is a very good saying within recovery groups: 'You cannot blame (or thank) the *people, places, and things* for your happiness.' Only *you* can make *you* happier.

It is very freeing and quite a relief to know that the power is yours, right here, right now, to make yourself happy. Just stop wanting other stuff. Just be happy right now with exactly what you have and exactly who you are.

Now, I'm not saying that if you are in a bad job or a bad marriage, you should stay in it. You should use your boundaries and try to make changes, and if it is not possible to continue, then you should make the necessary arrangements to change your situation.

But most of us are not in that situation all the time. Most of the time, we just don't have everything we think we need or want right now, so we make ourselves quite unhappy while we wait for it.

Also, I know we all have to do tasks that we just do not want to do sometimes, or things happen to us that we are just not happy about.

So, we do what the dog did. We do the unpleasant task/or feel the unpleasant feeling at the time that we have to do it (like when the toy hit his head), and then we just get back to the good stuff. He did not dwell on his sore head; he just got excited about the next great thing that was put in front of him.

I heard it put very simply the other day: 'Just do it when it has to be done, and then put it out of your mind when you are not doing it.'

I once read a story about two young brothers. Their mum was taking them on a day trip to the zoo. They were both very excited about the trip, and in the morning, they jumped in the car full of excitement and anticipation of the event ahead. Now, one brother sat on the edge of his seat the whole way there. 'How long till we get there, Mum?' 'I'm hungry! Will we eat on the way?' 'My legs are cramped. Is it far away?' 'What time will we get there? Is it halfway yet?'

However, the other brother sat comfortably and rested on the back of the seat. He looked out the window and enjoyed the view. He saw newborn lambs, and he made games up out of counting how many red cars he saw or which was the biggest hay bale. He hummed his favourite tunes from *Sesame Street* to himself as he sat quietly.

Now, of course both brothers got to the zoo at the same time and enjoyed a fabulous day with all the animals and the company of their mum; but as a whole, who enjoyed the day more? And more importantly, if the car had broken down along the way and they had had to call the NRMA, have it re-started, and return home without a trip to the zoo, which would have still enjoyed his day? The answer, of course, is the brother who had *enjoyed the journey.*

I think this story is a great one for showing us that we can all enjoy the journey of life right now as it is happening, no matter whether the things that we hope for ahead of us are even better than what we have now.

I recently visited Fiji for a holiday. Now, this is a country that is full of natural beauty, and so its biggest industry is tourism. The resorts there are absolutely astoundingly beautiful and are literally heaven on earth. Perhaps you have not lived until you have walked on the white, sun-warmed beaches of one of Fiji's smaller islands and had a gorgeous, dark-skinned Fijian islander walk towards you with a freshly picked frangipani and place it behind your ear, saying, 'A beauty for a beauty' as he smiles that grand Fijian smile . . . . Oh, but I digress . . . .

My point is that even though these people live in one of the most beautiful places on earth, it is actually a third world country. The majority of the population live in poverty like I have never seen in my life.

And do you know what is amazing about this? Fiji is known to have the happiest people in the world. And it's not just the tag line for their national airline; it is actually the truth. These people, who often live without electricity, running water, or windows and floors in the huts, will still run to the side of the road to wave at you and say *'Bula!'* (welcome!), just because they mean it.

When was the last time someone came running out of a multi-million dollar house in the suburbs in Australia just to wave 'Welcome!' when you drove past?

This makes you think, doesn't it? Happiness does not come from the things you have; it comes from inside of you.

Now, this is not to say that the Fijians are quite content with their lot in life; they are not. They are all very keen to work hard and will take just about any work that is offered them so that they can make some money to provide for their families. However, while they work towards their goal, they are still *happy now.* If they waited until they got rich enough to put floors on their huts, unfortunately, most of them would die very unhappy, because most of them will not end up with floors on their huts. In the meantime, they are *happy.*

My favourite definition of happiness is this: *To be happy is having someone to love, something to do, and something to look forward to.* Nowhere in that sentence does it mention that we need to be rich to be happy.

All of the thoughts and feelings related to fear are based in the future as we think of what might happen, and everything related to anger and resentment sits in our past as we look back. *To rid ourselves of feelings of fear, anger, and resentment, all we need to do is live in the present,* and we will find happiness right now.

We can take a leaf out of the book of the *happiest animal on earth* and the *happiest people on earth* and know that the key to true happiness is to *live in the moment.*

Charm 8:

Yesterday is history. Tomorrow is a mystery. Today is a gift. That's why it's called the present.

Chapter 9

There Is No Finish Line

(Perfection)

Perfection is not an oasis; it is a mirage.
—Author Unknown

As the lesson on happiness started to 'sit' with me, I began to wonder about what it was exactly that I had been trying to achieve with all my hard work for all these years. I was having a coffee with Anne one day when we pondered this question. I told Anne that it had become very apparent to me that I had been working so hard to achieve happiness. She asked, 'What did you think your version of happiness was, Sharon? What have you been working for?'

I knew the answer. The answer was perfection for myself and my life. I had been working for nothing less than perfection.

I believed perfection was an achievable goal that I could, and obviously should, work for.

For me, perfection was to 'have it all'. Perfect marriage, perfect kids, perfect house, perfect parties, perfect business, perfect bank account—and I was to do it without a hair out of place. A little bit *Stepford Wives,* don't you think?

At this time, I saw my life in absolutes. I thought everything was fixed; there was no room for flexibility. I used to think like this:

- I must *never* let anything bad happen to my family.
- I must *always* do my best.
- I must *never* let my children down.

It never *occurred* to me that this was an unachievable goal. As usual, I assumed that if I worked hard enough, tried harder, and did more for everyone, then at some stage, all these things would actually all be done. I thought there was some kind of a finish line when life would be perfect.

In the meantime, I did not take the time to stop and smell the roses. I was not enjoying life because I was so busy working towards perfection in all these areas of my life that it did not even seem relevant to take pleasure in the joys that life was offering me each and every day.

So, what is the definition of perfect, anyway?

I believe there are two types of perfection that many of us are working towards:

- aesthetics (how we and our loved ones look), and
- actions (what we and our loved ones do).

'So,' Anne said, 'you think that when something is perfect, it is finished?'

'Well, um, yes,' I replied, realizing as soon as the words left my mouth that this was a ridiculous concept.

Right then, I had a moment of realization that I did not *want* to be finished yet.

I realized that learning lessons in life, growing, changing, and maturing were what it was all about.

Life was the *journey* not the *finish line*.

And so, if life is the journey, then when you think about it, we are actually perfect all the time because we are perfect for what we are and what we are supposed to be doing *right now*. God, or the Universe, does have a plan, and really at no time will we understand what that plan is for us.

As I sat and discussed this concept further with Anne, I said, 'I understand that God has a plan for me, but I just wish that I could see the plan, check the plan, and approve the plan before God put it into place.'

'No,' she said, 'that is the point. What we are doing now is perfect based on the information we know right now.'

I now always remember that although I don't understand what the plan is, I do know that whoever I am right now and whatever I am doing right now are perfect for right now.

So the paradox of perfection is that by realizing that there is no single time that perfection will be achieved, I achieve perfection all the time just by being me, right now, as I am.

There is only one me, and there only ever will be, and I am doing *me* perfectly, right now.

So if you are searching for perfection in what you *own,* then I can tell you this for sure: if you try to own the nicest house, there will always be someone with a nicer house than you. If you try to buy the fastest car, there will be someone whose car is faster. If you try to buy the biggest high-definition TV, then tomorrow they will invent a better one, and most likely your most envious next-door neighbour will buy it.

And if you are searching for some kind of perfection in how you look, if you think you need to look like someone you saw in a magazine or a movie, then you need to know that the world would be a really boring place if we all looked the same! You look perfect for you, because remember, there is only *one* you. Don't try to be a perfect someone else—be an awesome you!

If the motivation behind getting, buying, or doing something is to be perfect at it, then you will never, ever be happy, as you will never achieve that goal. It is an unachievable goal. *It is like trying to get to the supermarket on a treadmill: it is never going to happen.*

One more very important pitfall in aiming for some kind of unachievable perfection is that mostly we know, deep down in our hearts, that this goal is unreachable, and so the danger becomes that we do not even try to achieve anything because we know that we cannot do it to perfection. The old saying 'better to have tried and failed than to never have tried at all' rings true here.

Many years ago, when Simon and I were running the accounting firm, I remember we used to listen to the cassette tapes (yes, cassette tapes—it was pre-CD!) of Nick Murray, who was at that time known to be one of the world's premier financial planners. Nick used to say often, 'I love it when customers say *no! This* is because I know that one out of every ten customers says yes! So, every time I get a no, I am closer to the yes!'

So remember that even though you may feel like you have not done *perfectly,* you have in fact tried something and got a no, and so you move closer to your yes!

A fabulous way to check your progress towards being an awesome *you* is to track your progress every day. Some people journal; other people do a mental list each night. Either way, you need to congratulate yourself for all the things you have done to the best of your ability that day, and also make note of the things you could have done differently and whether there is anyone you need to apologise to for that. Then get up the next day without guilt (guilt is a wasted emotion) and start again on your quest towards the best you that you can be.

I took this new-found information that Anne had shared with me and incorporated it into my life almost immediately. Someone had said to me years ago that the best thing you could do for your kids was, once they were physically able to do something, allowing them to do it. Allow them to make their own mistakes and to do it their way. Well, the old me was never going to do this, as the kids would not do it *perfectly.*

However, that night, when I went home from coffee with Anne and our discussion about perfection, I told my kids that now that they were twelve years old, they were capable of using a push-button washing machine as easily as I was, so from now on, they could do their own washing. I did this without anger and without guilt (amazingly), and Josie and Jackson's response was 'Cool, at least now you won't be harassing us about putting our clothes in the clothes basket.'

So, from that day on, my children have done their own washing. And it is not perfect.

I made Anne proud that day as I moved on through my journey to learn that the less I expected perfection from myself, the more I accepted the imperfections in others, which in itself began to bring me joy.

Charm 9:

Our life's journey is progress, *not* perfection.

Chapter 10

There Are No Contracts

(Acceptance)

Living is like writing a book: it involves tearing up one rough draft after another.

—Anonymous

Coming into eighteen months of sobriety, I was really starting to get a handle on the importance of emotional growth, on letting go of my fears and my need to be perfect in order to live a happy and joyful life. But as part of this process, I was getting hung up on what had happened in my past, and also on the cards that life had handed me. Apart from anything else, alcoholism is a chronic (that means incurable) disease that I wake up with every single day. Many alcoholics in recovery have reminded me over the years that even though I am not drinking, my disease is just outside in the car park doing push-ups, gaining its strength in case ever I call it back into the house. Like so many other people, I was getting caught up in my past, and it was preventing me from moving forward.

When I was five years old (rumour has it that this event happened on the actual day of my fifth birthday), my father left our family.

I don't recall the fighting; I just remember him not being there anymore.

And my father really *left*. We did not get any birthday cards or Christmas gifts; no phone calls; he was just gone. Now, my parents of course have different versions of what happened and why we never saw him (and I understand this because there are always two sides to each story). Suffice it to say that I did not see my father for another thirty-two years.

This separation from my father left me feeling that I had an unfair disadvantage in life.

At this time in my recovery, I realized that many of us feel like this—like life has given us some kind of unfair disadvantage. Some people feel like this because of things that happened to them during childhood; for other people, it is because of events that have unfolded for them as adults.

The big question is, why did we think it was unfair? What made us think that life should be giving us anything different from what we were given?

It was at this time that I searched out and read some books about acceptance. I needed to learn how to accept what life had given me and go forward. Interestingly enough, it was at this time that I met a newly sober alcoholic, Janine. Discussions with Janine began to make me realize that I needed to learn how to accept everything that life had given me, the good and the bad, in order to go forward.

You see, Janine had one of the worst stories I had ever heard. Janine had had abuse of all kinds in her life. She had had emotional and sexual abuse in her family of origin, she had been involved in a very bad marriage early on in her life, and she had a life full of mental torture and physical violence. Her story ended in prison after she finally lashed back at one of her abusers. Janine was at a place in her life where she could have been full of anger, hate, and revenge. However, acceptance had been one of the lessons that Janine had had to learn on her journey of emotional growth. She had realized that no matter how bad the things were that had happened to her (and they were bad), no matter how unfair it was that these things had happened to her (and it was unfair), she *must accept* them as part of who she was in order to move forward. If she sat in hatred, anger, and revenge she would never, ever be able to move forward.

Apart from the fact that what had happened in Janine's life made any problem in my life seem trivial, it also became very clear to me that it does not matter what level of unfair stuff has happened in our lives; we can live with it if we *accept* it.

I believe that there are a whole lot of assumptions we make about what life should give us, and we begin to feel unfairly done by if these things do not pan out exactly like we expect.

Two of the first assumptions that we misguidedly make are that our parents have the ability to love us unconditionally and that they have the ability to show us. Unfortunately, a key lesson to learn here is that parents are only human. They always, always do the best they know how to do and that is all you can ask or expect from them. Like everyone, parents do not get out of bed in the morning with the intention of making bad decisions that will affect you adversely. Our parents, like us, are going through a journey of emotional growth, and they can only do what they think is right at the time they do it. Sometimes, that will leave with adverse outcomes that *do* affect your life. We need to *accept* that our parents are doing the best they *know* how to do *at that time.*

The next expectation that we often have in life is that if we love the person we marry, make sacrifices, and work hard, then we will be able to stay married, and happily married at that, forever. Unfortunately, if this does not turn out how we expected, we often feel unfairly done by, again. There are so many reasons why a relationship can break up and/or run its course, and sometimes those things cannot be fixed, no matter how hard we work. Some relationships *do* last forever; however, many do not. We need to accept that relationships can change and there is *no guarantee* that your relationship will last forever, no matter how hard you work.

It is also a common belief that if we work hard in business or as employees, then we will be rewarded financially. Now, I am the first to say that the old saying 'the harder I work, the luckier I become' very often holds true. But unfortunately, sometimes it does not, and we cannot *expect* it to be always true. It is true, of course, that we cannot sit on our butts and do nothing and expect great things from life either, but there are no guarantees that wealth will come with hard work.

Being the over-functioner that I was for so many years, I did work very hard at home and in the business that I had with my husband. Now, as it happens, the decisions made by my husband and me did pay off financially, and our hard work was very worthwhile. However, it does not always turn out like that for everyone. Having been in business for many years now, I have seen many, many people who have put their lives and souls into their own small businesses. Many times, it does not leave them with the financial security that equals the level of effort they have put into the business. They thought that if they worked hard, they would make good money, but again, they are left feeling unfairly done by. There are so many variables in business that we need to know that sometimes, no matter how hard we work, we may be left financially unrewarded for our work.

I have also felt very unfairly done by when people have stolen from me. It is hard to imagine when you start with nothing, when you work hard, when you pay taxes and transact business honestly, that people would steal from you. When this happens, it does feel unfair. It is one thing when it happens randomly, like when our house was broken into and the thieves took every electrical item they could carry from the house with them. I did handle this better because it is random. However, I find it very difficult to understand when it is targeted stealing. By this I mean when someone knows it is my business and that I am a small independent business owner and they think it is okay to steal from me. This is because I have made the mistake of thinking that everyone else's truths and values are the same as mine, when they are not. We need to remember that *bad things do happen to good people.*

So why do we feel like life is unfair?

I believe it is because we think there is some kind of invisible contract between us and the universe or God, a contract that says we should always get what we deserve and perhaps a bit of extra stuff that we don't! We are often left feeling like the universe has not held up its end of the contract.

Here is the very important message in this lesson. *There is no contract.* I repeat, *there is no contract.*

There is only acceptance. Remember that we can only ever be responsible for our reaction to a situation. We cannot have control over the outcome itself, and we cannot change other people's behaviour.

I am not talking about accepting a bad situation and staying in it. I am talking about accepting that it has happened to you and making your best decision to go forward. Do this each and every step of your life. Accept what has happened, and move forward.

Let me put another idea to you about the universe. Perhaps the universe has a plan for us all, and it is not always actually what we expect it to be. Sometimes (well, most of the time), that can be quite disconcerting, as we all like to know that we have a plan for our lives and that is how it is going to work out. Now, I'm all for having some kind of plan for our lives, and I, for one, could not get out of bed in the morning if I did not have a reason to get up. However, here's a tip: we need to be really adaptable and accept that things will happen differently from what we expect. We always have those two choices: we can kick and scream and think that life is unfair, or we can accept that these things have happened, do the next right thing, and leave the outcome to the universe.

Here's an analogy that I find helpful to get my head around this concept.

You are on your life's journey, and each day, all you can see are the roads directly in front of you, beside you, and behind you. It does not matter which direction you turn or how hard you look into the horizon; you can still only see what is directly in front of you.

However, the universe has a 'bird's eye view' of your journey. The universe can see the *whole* map, right to the end of your life's journey. It can see all the roadblocks along the way and all the bumps in the road. Sometimes, the universe will let you hit a bump (even though it knows a way you could have got around it) and lets you learn how to heal yourself. Once you have learned that lesson and know how to heal yourself faster, it will prepare you for a bigger bump that may lie ahead later in life. So, when you think you've been unfairly done by and you think your deal with the universe has been broken, remember that there was *no contract,* and that this was just part of your journey.

Which leads me back to my father.

Finally, after spending thirty-two years feeling unfairly done by because my father had not held up his part of my imaginary contract, I asked a private detective to find him.

'You know, Sharon, that most fathers who have ceased contact with their kids do not want to be found,' the private detective informed me.

'I know, but I am ready for the closure now, so let's get it over and done with,' was my honest reply.

Two days later, I received a phone call from the detective, who told me that much to his surprise, he had found my father and that he was very keen to meet me and had been waiting all these years for one of us to call.

Now, I will not say that I understand this, and right to this day, I am not sure why he did not make contact with us or why he left us all those years to feel unloved by him. (Don't worry—I think my mum made up for it with double-lovin'.) But this was a great lesson in accepting what my father was able to give at that time.

My father is now a part of our lives and the lives of most of my family. He has said numerous times that he has learned a lot since that time when he left us and that he would have done things differently given the chance again. But what I do know now is that he did the best he knew how to do at the time. So, on his return to our lives, I had two choices. Either I could carry the grudge of the imaginary contract that I felt had been unfulfilled all this time, or I could get on and build a current relationship with him and base it on all the good and bad times that would happen within our relationship from that time onwards.

So, after Janine had shown me, through the power of her own story, how I needed to accept in order to grow and be happy, I asked her how she managed that on a day-to-day basis. How do you 'un-see' what your eyes have seen?

She told me that her life-saving tool was gratitude.

Acceptance and gratefulness go hand in hand. She said that she had learnt to make it part of her day to be grateful for what she now had in life, big and small.

When Janine mentioned this concept to me, I realized I had not been grateful for much in my life and I had no idea where to start. So I started with being grateful for waking up, then for having clean air to breathe and food to eat, and I went on from there. Now even when the worst part of any day or week or month is upon me, I find gratefulness in each situation, even if it is only that I am learning and growing from the pain. Practising grateful behaviours was a turnaround point in my life and towards living a joyful life. The more I practiced being grateful for, the more I realized how many things I have to be grateful for. Living gratefully can be life-changing and will definitely help you to learn the value of acceptance.

So, remember that the only certain thing in life is really very simple: *You were born, and you will die.* Absolutely everything else is changeable, and there is *no contract* that says otherwise.

If you want a guarantee, buy a toaster!

Charm 10:

It is what it is.

Chapter 11

Off with the Fairies

(Finding God)

I know God will not give me anything I can't handle. I just wish that He didn't trust me so much.

—Mother Teresa

Learning the lesson of acceptance started me thinking on how many things had happened to me that no matter how much I had tried to manage, I actually had no control over. During this time, I started to wonder, 'Who, then, has control?'

From when I was quite young, I 'knew' there was no such thing as God. It appeared quite obvious to me that the whole idea of an old man in the sky, white beard and all, did not seem to be very realistic, and it by no means had any connection to anything that was happening in my life.

By the time I was a young adult and well into my drinking and codependency, I was really sure that there was no God. I was an atheist, someone who has no belief in any god. A belief in God and a really good dose of codependency have trouble coexisting. It is very difficult to believe that you have the power to fix everything for everyone while at the same time thinking that there is a God out there that can do it too.

So imagine my surprise, perhaps peppered with a little anger, when the word *God* kept appearing in my conversations with many of these wise long-time alcoholics.

Another paradox of recovery was being put right in front of me. They were saying that a control-freak alcoholic would need to *let go* of control in order to get sober. This seemed to me to be the hardest solution to the most difficult problem. I wondered if there wasn't an easier way, one that I could control?

For me, the answer was no. The key to so many of my problems— alcoholism, codependency, control, fear—sat in my inability to *let go*.

By this stage, I knew that changes in my beliefs and behaviours would in the long run bring me substantial benefits, so I was willing to listen to people who I could see had something that I did not yet understand. I did not even know what I did not know yet; I did not know what they had, but I wanted it. And something deep down inside me knew that I needed this thing in order to stay sober, let alone to fix all the other issues in my life.

Once again, I drew on Anne's wisdom in search of a solution. Anne and I never met in dark and dingy smoke-filled cafés in the back streets, as you would expect of two drunks whispering about the answers to sobriety. We always met in one of the modern, cool-coloured cafés filled with natural light and a buzz of gentle laughter. It suited our journey and the people we had become more. So, as we sat in the café this day, the large modern chandelier twinkling as the sun hit it above our table, I asked Anne, 'What do I have to do to start on this journey that obviously brings peace to so many people?'

Her answer was simple, and perhaps it is the one sentence that is the answer to every single question. She said, 'Give it up to God.'

If this sentence makes the hairs on the back of your neck stand on end with fear, as it did with me, then you probably need to learn this as much as I did. Even if it scares you, just read on and see if there is anything here for you.

I found that the first thing to do was *forget everything I had ever learned about God*, and find my own.

This concept was absolutely life-changing for me.

It had never occurred to me that God could ever be anything other than what someone else had already thought of. This is where I became aware of the clear distinction between religion and spirituality. Until this time, I had thought that if I was to believe in a god, any god, I would need to do it in the structured environment of a religion.

There is a big difference between learning to live with spirituality for emotional growth and spiritual development, on the one hand, and living with religion for the prevention of eternal damnation, on the other.

I have heard it said that religion is for people who fear going to hell, but spirituality is for people who have already seen, or lived through, hell on earth.

My alcoholism was hell on earth, which is maybe why I was open to the idea of finding my own God if that could help me.

I now understand that spirituality is to live as a directly God-related spiritual being. Spirituality can be practiced with or without the affiliation to a religion.

In order to do this, though, we must have a belief that God, or some kind of higher power, does *actually* exist.

I found this very difficult in the beginning, as I had no idea what my God-concept even was. I found that it is harder to accept there is a god than to act like God.

Shortly after that meeting with Anne, I met William, who was about eight years sober. He told me to think of it like this: 'Sharon, you are the lamp, and God is the electricity. It was always there to help you work properly; you just have to plug it in.'

He went on to explain to me that I was able to use whatever God concept worked for me. I just had to make some kind of connection with a higher power.

I asked William how he had done this. William was another person who, like Janine, had a really horrific story from his childhood. Unfortunately, some of his abuse was within the walls of a structured religion, so he actually did believe in God when he came in to recovery, but he believed that his God had forsaken him in order for these atrocities to happen to him. So William went on to explain how he had been through the process of stripping back everything that he had been taught in his past about God, as he was, understandably, unable to reconcile the God he had been taught about and the things that had happened to him. William had gone through this process of un-learning everything he had learnt and literally started fresh. He learned to meditate (his own version of prayer), and he just left himself open to seeing God's actions when they were shown to him in his everyday life. William now has a very strong God-connection to his own concept of his higher power. I could see that I could use the wisdom William had shown me to start finding my own God.

I asked around to see what people had as their God-concept. It was wide and varied.

For some people, it was nature. For others, it was the moon, stars, and sun. A number of people said it was the beauty of a sunrise. For a lot of people, it is simply the universe.

Perhaps the most memorable God I have heard about was from my friend who very strongly believes that God is a 'she'—a feminine and gentle Goddess whose matriarchal blessings my friend likes to see as a *pink fairy*.

To me, this showed that it didn't matter what God looked like. It just mattered that God is like gravity—no one knows what it is, but because its effects are evident, we know it is there.

The important lesson I learned from these people, with their wide variety of God-concepts, is that to live with spirituality, it actually does not matter what your concept of God is, as long as it works for you.

As long as you believe that there is a higher power, then you will have the ability to let go of the control and have *faith*.

For some people, it can actually be a bit harder if they already have a God concept and are part of a structured religion currently, or it was strong in their childhood. I believe that if your God, or your current religion, is not working for you, then you have the ability to change it. If you can't find answers in your current religion, then look for what works for you. You may need to clear away your old thoughts, like clearing a building site before the building begins, just as William had to do.

The true key to *letting go* is in having a really good connection with your God. All of us have the ability to find that connection with God. We do not need a special building (church) to do it in, and we do not need religious leaders to stand between us and our God.

Your distance from God is directly related to the anxiety you feel.

I had to check my progress on my journey towards a higher power many times with William, Anne, and many other people I had met whom I believed had a good recognition of their God. Right after my discussion with William, I met again with Anne to ask her, 'How do I get this connection with my God?'

I think I knew the answer of course. It was prayer.

And so I began to pray, and I began to clear away all the old beliefs I had about what God was. It was not an overnight process, and my God concept has evolved quite significantly since I first started praying. Finding my own God has changed my life enormously. I don't need to sing and dance about my God belief to anyone else. I don't need to put my daily religious quote on my Facebook page to convince anyone else that *my* God should be *their* God. I am just quietly living a spiritual life, and I have given up control to my God. And all I needed to do to get this kind of life-changing enlightenment was to begin to pray.

Prayer can come in many forms, and like the word *God,* it can have negative connotations for some people. As with so many of the beliefs that come with a religious upbringing, many of us think that we need to kneel down, head bowed, hands clasped, before we can begin to pray to God. I do not believe this is true. I believe we can, and should, talk to God all the time, lots of times, anywhere we are.

Meditation is an excellent way to begin building your connection to God. There are so many advantages to meditation, not the least of which is that you are more likely to hear God speak to you if you are listening.

I strongly believe that God is shown to us all day, every day, in the faces of the people we see and talk to. With each lesson you need to learn, God is showing you the answer all the time through the voices of the people around you; you just have to listen. So listen well. Listen to the people whom God puts in your path each and every day. See if they are there today to show or tell you something that you should be listening to.

Many of our religious beliefs that we were taught from childhood also lead us to believe that God will reward people for good behaviour and punish those for bad behaviour. I don't know that to be true, although sometimes it appears that way, and it also appears like bad things happen to good people. This is true—they do. The important thing here to remember is that God has a plan that we just do not understand, and we are not meant to.

Imagine you are travelling on a journey, by car, from Sydney to Perth. You start your journey at night. You get in your car, and you turn on your headlights, and off you go. Although your headlights shine bright, they do not show you all the way to Perth; they only allow you to see a couple of hundred meters ahead of you. Do you stop your journey because you cannot see all the way? No, you carry on *with faith.* You know that you can only make decisions based on the two hundred meters you can see ahead of you, but you know you will make it to Perth if you make the right decisions that are put in front of you each time. Spiritual wisdom is not to *understand* what God's plan is; it is to *accept* God's plan.

To that end, I believe there is really only one prayer that we should all be praying to God:

'God, please let me see your *will* for me today.'

That's it. Ask it all the time, and then *look* for it. If you are going to sit around and wait for a lightning bolt, then you will probably be left somewhat un electrified. God's directions to you are more likely to be much more subtle and frequent. Remember, God will keep showing you those pebbles (answers) in everyone you meet and see today, so keep a really good eye out for them. Look into the faces of every person you see today, and look for the answer to your one and only prayer, because the answer will be there.

I have a mobile phone that allows words to come up, to look like a text message, when an alarm goes off. I have set the alarm that goes off every morning, and it appears like a text message that says,

> Message from God. Good morning! I have your day under control; there is no need for you to get involved. Have a great day.

So, if you do not already have one that works for you, go out and start looking for your God. There is no right way or no wrong way, but there is *a* way for you. Clear your building site, and be prepared to build a God-house that will change your outlook on life as it has done for mine.

Charm 10:

No God, no peace.
Know God, know peace.

Chapter 12

The Sheep Fence and Mother-Guilt

(Boundaries)

Your current safe boundaries were once your unknown frontiers.

—Anonymous

I was heading towards the end of my second year of sobriety, and I had accepted so many new lessons into my life that I was starting to see *real* changes in the way each day in my life panned out. I lived through my fears every day; I lived with gratefulness; and I was learning to live in the moment much more than I ever had before. All of these things were allowing me to get small pockets of joy and happiness within each day. However, I was still in large amounts of emotional pain, and I knew that I still had things to learn—or at least I hoped I did, or else I would have to live in this much pain forever.

I remember now, in hindsight, that at that time, Anne pointed out to me that all the changes I had made so far were completely personal. I had not asked anything of anyone else in my life, and I had not really asked for any changes from my friends or family. 'To that extent, Sharon, you are still over-functioning,' she explained to me. 'You are going to have to get to the stage where you put some boundaries in place with the people in your lives, even the ones you love.'

As I had no idea what she was talking about, I nodded my head in agreement, as I had done before. But inside my mind, I was thinking, *How can asking other people to do things, especially my family, help how I feel?* I was still of the opinion that I could fix everything, sort everything, and make everyone happy. Asking someone else to do something was not the solution I thought I was looking for.

Not long after this conversation, I was speaking to my counselor about the pain that I was still feeling. 'Sharon,' he said, 'I think it is time you did some reading on boundaries and put some boundaries in place in your life.' I must have had quite a puzzled look on my face, as he said, 'Sharon, do you know what boundaries are?'

'Of course,' I replied. 'They are the fences around a sheep farm to keep all the sheep from getting out.'

I may laugh now, but that was actually the extent of my knowledge of what a boundary was. I now know that there are physical boundaries, like fences and walls, and then there are emotional boundaries. As Anne and my counselor suggested, I started doing some reading on boundaries.

Put simply, a boundary is knowing when to say yes and how to say no.

Unlike a wall which is built to keep people out and to protect yourself, an emotional boundary is for your values and standards of what is acceptable for you and your situation.

Like so many women, I had absolutely no idea how to say no. I never said no. In fact, people did not even get to the stage where they had to ask me—I had probably already done it!

I started practising my boundaries in the same place I had practised everything else, in my coffee mornings with other recovering alcoholics. It was like my kindergarten school for life, so it was a great place to practice everything. I did not feel like these people would reject me, so I could try out my new skills as I learnt them.

One of the boundary 'tests' went like this. One woman, Alyssa, had asked me if we could meet for coffee on our own during the week to discuss her situation, because she thought there was something I could help with. 'Sure,' I agreed, and we arranged a time and place. The day of the meeting arrived, and she cancelled one hour before, pretty much without reason, so we re-arranged the coffee date for another day and time. Second time around, and the same thing happened with her cancelling at short notice. This time, I was going to set a boundary. 'Alyssa, I am happy to make another time for us to meet, but it has been inconvenient for me to make arrangements and then have you cancel twice. If you are unable to get to this appointment, I will not be able to re-schedule again.' Although this may appear trivial, it is not, because a lot of women would *not* put this boundary in place. They would continue to say yes and arrange their day, time and time again, around an appointment that probably would not happen. We want to be *helpful and kind,* and often, putting boundaries in place does not make us feel like this.

I then went on to start putting boundaries in place with other people in my life, like extended family and friends, and then worked my way up to the three most important people in my life. I started with small boundaries so I made sure I could stick to them, like 'Josie, please put your plate in the dishwasher or you will need to wash the dishes by hand' through to 'Jackson, pick up that toy off the floor within the next half hour or I will confiscate it for a week.' I then went on to the ones that actually caused me pain, like 'Simon, it hurts me when you make fun of my choices in front of your parents. If you do that again, I will no longer be able to attend your family's functions.'

Now, I don't want you to think that practicing these boundaries was easy, because it was not. It is a simple concept, but it is not easy. It was difficult for me to even put the simplest boundary in place, and it was downright painful to put the difficult ones in place. And the guilt nearly killed me. If I was ever going to pick up a drink, it was probably going to be over the guilt.

Now, the good news about emotional boundaries is that you are in charge of your own boundaries. No boundary is right or wrong—it's *your* boundary.

But the bad news is that if you have hardly ever, or never, used emotional boundaries, then it does take quite a lot of practice until you can use them freely and it starts to feel normal.

After you have done some reading on boundaries and are ready to try them out, I strongly suggest that you do not try them on someone who is important to you! Start with an insignificant relationship about an unimportant issue. 'Why bother?' you may ask. Because you will need practice, and lots of it.

Setting up boundaries sounds easy, and it is a very, very simple concept; but it is quite difficult to implement into your relationships, especially if you have been without boundaries until now.

Do not apply a boundary to another person in anger. Do not speak rudely, meanly, or unfairly to another person. In fact, you will find that your boundaries are much more likely to be well received when you do them gently and without anger in your voice (even if it is something you care very deeply about and you are angry about).

It is always very important to remember that your boundaries are not meant to change or control another person. Your boundaries are not to be used as a threat; they are only to be used to make clear what is *acceptable to you*. The outcome of a boundary is to make clear to the other person what you need in the relationship.

It is also important to know that you do not need to apologise for the way you feel. Other people will feel differently from you; oftentimes, they will not understand why you want to put that boundary in place, especially if it is not important to *them*. Just remember, it is *your* boundary, and you are allowed to feel the way you feel. It is not selfish to put a healthy boundary in place, and another person's feelings are no more important than your own. I will repeat that point because it is often missed, especially by women. *No one else's feelings are any more (or less) important than your own.*

Once you make a boundary, you *must stick to it! Do not*, I repeat, *do not* start trying out your boundaries until you are ready to stick to them. That is why it is *so* important to start with unimportant issues and with people that you are not in a primary relationship with.

Another very, very important pitfall to be prepared for is that most people will 'fight back' when boundaries are set.

Whatever they have been doing up until now has been working for them, at least on some level (otherwise they would not have been doing it), so they will not want to change (otherwise they would have done it already). They will often try to tell you that you are wrong to require that boundary, they will often belittle you, and they will often try to convince you that your values and ideas are wrong or insignificant. Remember, for the most part, they are afraid, so they will be responding in fear, and that is the least constructive place to respond from. That is why you must be secure in your boundary before you bring it up with them.

A great, and very common, example of this is a codependent spouse of an alcoholic or addict.

Say a friend of yours has an alcoholic husband. She comes to you regularly and complains about how terrible he is: how he comes home drunk all the time, never looks after the kids, and wastes all their money. She knows that she is enabling him and that she should kick him out and tell him he will be welcome back when he has sobered up.

Your friend has not done that yet, and she continues to pay his bills, clean up after him, and even buy his beer for him as she continues to complain to you about her lot in life.

Although she is clearly codependent and needs to work on her own self-care for the wellbeing of herself and her children, the role of martyr and all-round *good wife* is still working for her on some level, or she would change it. And she is obviously not well-versed in setting her own boundaries, or your friend would already have set them with her husband.

So, since you are unable to hear her talk about it when she obviously has no intention of changing it, it is time for you to set a boundary about your part in the relationship. You cannot make your friend change her own boundaries, and remember, it is not your job to do it. It is absolutely okay for you to set a boundary about her complaining to you about it.

You can set your boundary by explaining to your friend that you care about her and you will be willing to help her with whatever she needs should she decide to separate from her husband until he sobers up. However, you explain to her that you find it unbearable to hear of the damage the relationship is doing to her in the meantime. You say that you do not want to talk about her husband when you are together or you will have to avoid your regular get-togethers.

This example clearly shows how you can put your own boundary in place without asking other people to change behaviours they are not yet ready to change.

Emotionally healthy people will accept good boundaries and have boundaries of their own. Unfortunately, you may lose some of your relationships as a result of establishing boundaries, but the remaining relationships that are built on these boundaries will be happier and healthier.

One very regular stumbling block with setting boundaries is guilt. The guilt will really surprise you and may make you want to go back on the boundary. Don't let this catch you by surprise.

If you are anything like me, you are so used to people-pleasing that putting a boundary in place feels quite unusual. In the beginning, I did not know what to do with those feelings.

If the person I had applied the boundary to actually accepted my boundary request and there was a change in behaviour, then I would automatically feel guilty. And I hated to feel guilty. It was one of the worst feelings for me because I was so used to fixing everything for everyone. I thought that if I felt guilty, it meant I had not fixed something, so then I felt even more guilty! So when my guilt was brought on by a boundary that I had put in place, it was a lot for me to handle. But, like all of the lessons I have learnt, it got easier with practice.

The absolute worst of all guilt is mother-guilt. When you begin to put boundaries in place with your children, watch out for it, because mother-guilt is the worst kind there is. I found it almost too much to bear. We are so used to hearing that we must take away our children's pain and protect them at all costs; imagine my confusion when I was the one causing their discomfort!

This is the reason why I cannot stress how important it is for you to practice your boundaries with people whom you are least likely to feel guilty about and in relation to unimportant things. Practice until it becomes close to second nature to you before you begin on these important, and often painful, boundaries.

My boundaries are now so intertwined in the way I live my life that I am able to put boundaries in place, and stick to them, regularly and mostly without the feeling of guilt. In fact, this concept has worked so well for me that I find that if I do happen to find myself in pain now, it is generally because I have failed to put a good boundary in place.

Boundaries are well documented as the single best way for women to improve their lives, so build your boundary toolkit and work towards life-changing positive outcomes in your life too.

Charm 12:

Mean what you say, say what you mean, and don't say it meanly.

Chapter 13
Two Sides of the Velcro

(Codependency)

The most exhausting thing in life is to be insincere.

—Anne Morrow Lindbergh

So by this time in my recovery, I was well over my *honeymoon period*. Like most addicts in recovery, I thought that when I gave up my drug of choice (in my case, the grog), all my problems were going to go away. In the beginning, this was actually true, and in recovery terms, this is often called the honeymoon period.

At first, you start to feel physically better. No more throwing up all day, no more *mother of all headaches*, no more severe and constant liver pain. Lots of other problems start to go away too. You can stop lying to people so much (excuses about where you are when you are actually at home drinking). No more excuses about why you can't drive your kids around. A lot fewer arguments with the people around you, as most (if not all) of the arguments until now were alcohol-induced anyway.

I had made emotional changes in so many parts of my life. I had worked through so much of my fear, learned to feel my feelings, and made real progress on my emotional growth. Over this time, though, I started to realize that although I had made a lot of changes, I still had a long way to go; *the honeymoon period was over*. Although I had stopped drinking and was heading towards two years sober and it had become my full-time job to work on my recovery, I was still in so much pain, and I had no idea why.

In a way, this was an even more difficult moment than my gondola moment because now I was in a position where I still knew that I had everything that should make me happy (husband, kids, house, money, friends), I was not drinking anymore, and still something inside me was very, very wrong.

What was I missing? What was wrong? I began to realize that there was something very wrong in the relationship between Simon and me, and this was the key to my unhappiness. I didn't know what to do with this information in the beginning. My plan had always been to be in a happy marriage. I had worked, and was still working, so very hard to keep Simon happy. Wasn't that my definition of happiness? If Simon was happy, wasn't I supposed to be happy too?

I began to search for reading material that might help me with this quandary when I came across the word *codependency*. I think, like many of us, I had heard this term over the years in comedy shows and sitcoms, much like I had heard the word *addict,* and I had never thought either of these words pertained to me.

Then some things in my reading started to click. I started reading terms like *loved too much* and *subjugation,* and the stories in these books on codependency started to ring very true for me. I realized that codependency was another form of dealing with my unaddressed anxieties and that codependency could be affecting my life as badly as alcoholism had. I began to realize that this could be a big part of my problem, and I needed to know more.

And so I did something I had never done before: I spent a night away from Simon.

Yes, as crazy as this was, we had been together nearly twenty years and the only nights we had ever spent apart up until that time were enforced while I was in detox. As I was leaving detox, the staff there really, really wanted me to check into a longer-term rehabilitation centre in Sydney. We had the money for it, and there was in fact no reason for me *not* to go. In hindsight, it would have been the best thing ever for me, but at the time, I could not even contemplate spending those nights away from Simon. I now know that what I mistook for love was codependence.

So, with a spark of an idea that I might know why I was feeling the way I was, I jumped in the car and drove to Sydney to see the only woman I knew who would know the answer to this quandary: my friend Anne.

Anne, in her wisdom, had always been insightful in her method of sharing her wisdom with me. She would never outright come up with the answers for me, even though I think she always had them. She would wait patiently as I worked through my recovery process, and one at a time, I would come up with an issue, and she would then agree to help me find the solution to that emotional issue.

So on that day, as I had driven out of a cold Canberra winter day up to Sydney, I turned up on Anne's doorstep to blurt out, 'Anne, I think I'm codependent!'

She smiled, opened her arms, and said, 'Ah, I've been waiting for you to figure that one out. Come in, and we will work out what you can do from here. This one is going to be a big one, Sharon.'

So, 'What is codependency?' I hear you asking. There are many different definitions for codependency, and here is how I see it.

I see codependency as the need to put other people's happiness in front of your own to the detriment of yourself and the people around you. It is excessive care taking of another person and sacrifice, to the disadvantage of everyone involved. It is unhealthy to be on either end of a codependent relationship.

Here's how it played out for me.

Right from the beginning of my relationship with Simon, and then into the early years of our marriage, I just thought I was doing everything that a good wife was supposed to do. Haven't we all heard so many times about how marriage is all about sacrifice and about love being unselfish? I just thought that was what I was doing. I thought that in order to keep a marriage together, I would need to sacrifice.

As it was very important to me to keep my marriage together, I was happy to sacrifice what I wanted in order to have a happy marriage.

But as time went on, I started to forget what it was that I actually wanted or needed. What Simon wanted became what was important to us, and as the kids came along, the needs of the three of them became my number one priority, and in order to achieve that, I had to sacrifice my-*self*. I had subjugated my self, my needs, my values, my truths, for those I loved.

I would over-care for the three of them, and self-care was a nonexistent part of my life. I lived in guilt all the time—guilt that no matter how hard I worked, I could not care for them enough to take away their problems. Being an alcoholic and a codependent work quite well together, as I could self-medicate with my alcohol to get rid of the guilt for at least a while.

Somewhere in that time, I made some kind of switch from not only thinking that I should be putting their needs before my own, but also somehow feeling that I was responsible for their happiness.

That was the *big problem*.

I now know that no one can ever, ever, ever be responsible for another person's happiness. But in the midst of my codependency, I did not see that at all. I saw it as my failure if someone around me was unhappy. I would work long, hard, endless hours at work and at home to keep Simon and the kids happy. If they showed that they were unhappy, it made me angry because I could not fathom how they could possibly be unhappy when I was working so hard.

So if someone around me was unhappy, I would attempt to move heaven and earth to prevent that unhappiness next time. Of course, I know now that we all grow through our experiences and it is so very unfair for a codependent person to take away another person's opportunity for growth. It was very unfair of me to do this to Simon, and it was unfair of me to do it to my kids.

One of the hardest things I have had to learn how to do is to now watch my children go through painful growing experiences without trying to take away that pain for them. That is how my children will grow and mature (hopefully a lot quicker than I did) and remember that emotional pain will not actually kill them—it will, in fact, just make them stronger, just like the old saying says.

Recently, I was watching one of those reality shows on the telly (these are great shows to watch if you want to see a bit of emotional immaturity and see how far you've grown), and the teenage daughter was crying over something that had gone wrong for her at her prom night. The mother's response to the daughter's tears and sadness was to plead, 'Stop crying, Teagan! You are making me so upset with your sadness. Stop crying so I can be happy.' What the . . . ? The mother's first mistake was to make the daughter feel that she was responsible for her mother's happiness, and secondly, it is up to the mother to allow the daughter to *feel* her sadness, live through it, grow through it, and mature.

It is important to remember that we can not only be codependent with our spouses or our children; we can be codependent with our work, our family of origin (Mum, Dad, and siblings), our community (like your children's school), peer relationships, and friendships.

And in fact, I found that once you start with those codependent tendencies, you can often attempt to use your codependence to manage, and attempt to control, anxieties in all areas of life.

An important thing to remember is that you can only be codependent with someone who lets you.

Of course, children are an exception to this rule, as they are definitely not emotionally mature enough to tell you that you are over-parenting them; but for adults, this rule stands.

If the person on the other end of a potentially codependent relationship is healthy, they will use their boundaries (which of course they will have in place because they are healthy) to ensure that you understand that it is not your responsibility, or in fact even your place, to try to provide for their happiness. As they are healthy and emotionally mature, they know it is their own responsibility and in fact, their right, to provide for their own happiness.

They will not allow you to act codependently with them.

Which brings me to my words of warning if you have codependent tendencies. When it comes to relationships, it appears to me that the warped ideals of an active codependent work in perfect synergy with those of a narcissist or someone with narcissistic tendencies.

Narcissists *need* someone close to them who will feed their self-orientation as their overwhelming belief in the importance of their own self-care while the codependent needs to provide for the needs of the other person to the exclusion of his or her own self-care.

In short, they need to feel good, and you need to make them feel good.

You are like two sides of the Velcro, interlocking so tightly that neither of you can function alone. You are both, in fact, useless without the other side of your Velcro.

If you are heading towards, or have become, one side of a Velcro couple and you are in pain, I suggest that you take this opportunity to read the words of the very clever authors I have listed in the reading material at the end of the book. They will open your eyes to new ways of loving the people around you in a healthy, mature, and much less painful environment.

Growing out of codependency was a long and painful process for me. I was very scared when my initial reading said that it can take a long time to re-learn our codependent behaviours and start to see positive changes in our lives. I needed help, and I needed it now.

Once I had spoken to Anne and then went on to read everything I could get my hands on about codependency, I had to then make the very difficult next step of speaking to Simon about it, because this did involve him. I explained to Simon that I could see I was codependent, and I did not know what that meant for him or our relationship. I told him that I knew that I could not live in this kind of pain forever or I would inevitably pick up a drink. I needed to do some work in this area, and I knew it was going to change our relationship. I told him I had done a lot of reading in this area and I was going to speak to my counselor about it and see where it led me. To Simon's credit, he understood that this was an area that appeared to be affecting our relationship, and he agreed to see the counselor to speak about codependency also.

And what a journey this became!

I will not say it was pleasant; it was not. My codependency had become the central core that our relationship was built around. Learning the new behaviours involved in not acting or thinking co-dependently stripped our relationship down to its bare bones. We had to rethink the very basis of our relationship.

It was painful, as neither of us knew how to have a healthy relationship, healthy boundaries, or healthy behaviours towards each other.

Like a prisoner whose eyes hurt as she comes out of the darkness into the light, every step of working my way out of codependency hurt. Many times, I stepped back into the darkness of codependency just for its comfort of familiarity.

And so as I was heading into my third year of sobriety, the changes that freedom from codependency would bring me would change my life forever.

Charm 13:

You are not responsible for another person's happiness and the other person is not responsible for yours.

Chapter 14
Build Your Own Cake

(Be Yourself)

*The only success is to be able to live your life your
own way.*

—Christopher Morley

As I progressed through my journey away from codependency, it became clear how much I had morphed my life into Simon's over the last twenty years. And when I say my life, I mean my self. My actual *being*. Our lives were inseparable in that it was hard to tell where one of us finished and the other started.

We were having a party at our house around this time, and I remember being in one room having a conversation with two other people, Karl and Shane. Simon was in a different room. At one particular point, Karl was speaking to me when Simon came into the room we were in and joined the circle we were standing in. Then an amazing thing happened that I think had been happening for a long time, but on this day for the first time, I noticed it. As Simon moved into our group, no one said hello or made any comment to make note of the fact that he had entered. Karl, who had been speaking *directly* to me, just turned his head, mid-sentence, and continued the sentence with Simon as if I was no longer there. It was as if Karl thought that I was a stand-in for Simon until he got there, or more likely, that he saw us so much as one being that it didn't even occur to him to finish the sentence with me before going on to explain to Simon what he was talking about. I slipped silently away from the group without anyone noticing because the other half of me, the bigger half, was there now.

I was really peeved off. This was an ah-ha moment of clarity where I saw that I had become one half of a not-quite-whole. I needed to become a whole human being all on my own.

When Simon and I got married all those years ago, we were dead-set keen on making as much money as we could. I didn't really mind how we made the money, and I was willing to work hard to make the money. So we decided that we were going to put all our eggs in the one basket of Simon owning an accounting firm. It never occurred to me that we could actually work on separate dreams within the one family. I thought that to be a successful marriage and family, we would need to be working on the same goal together, always, forever.

So we were on a mission to get all that money and become *successful*. Our moneymaking occupation was the accounting firm. It never, ever, ever occurred to me that I should spend my days doing something that I enjoyed and try to make different money from what we were making together in the accounting firm.

I had only ever really had one thing I had ever enjoyed doing, and that was decorating cakes. Even though my drinking had got in the way of my pastry chef's apprenticeship, I really enjoyed the creative side of cake decorating, and I had continued to do it right through my life.

I taught myself a lot of the cake decorating skills, and my cakes got better and better over the years. Of course, being the over-functioner that I was, I would throw an *enormous* party for my twins' birthday every year. I'm talking *enormous*. Sixty to a hundred people, no problems. We built everything in our backyard to accommodate these huge parties, and I mean everything. We built a pirate ship (yes, a whole ship, including a wooden hull, sails, the whole lot) for the Peter Pan party; we built our own version of the Hogwarts train station for the Harry Potter party, steam train and all; we built a giant bed that took up the whole back yard for the *Toy Story* party. For every great party we held, I made a cake of suitable stature to honour these great events.

I was always the one who turned up with the cake at someone else's birthday, and of course, from quite early on, I was always the mum who was happy to provide cupcakes for hundreds of children at the school. But my passion for cakes was never thought of as anything other than a hobby, by me or by Simon.

As our accounting practice got busier and more successful, I fell more and more into Simon's shadow. At the time, of course, I did not realize that I was losing my *self* in the process of building Simon's *self*.

When I look back now, I see that I had become a small attachment alongside my larger-than-life husband.

The best way I can describe it is that Simon, being the ideas man, would throw all the proverbial balls in the air as he marched through his journey of life, and I would walk along behind him catching all the balls, sorting them into alphabetical order, delegating the task-balls, and then cleaning up the mess of the balls that I missed as they hit the floor with a thud.

People used to comment how lucky we were to spend all our time together, work and play. Simon's interests became my interests; my interests were delegated to negligible importance. Simon never forced any of this on me; I allowed it to happen because I did not value the importance of my own self.

All through the process of my self-minimization, I thought that I was doing what I ought to be doing to be a supportive wife.

I believe that this loss of my self was one of the key reasons for my unhappiness that led to my emotional rock bottom that day in the gondola.

When I got married, my marriage vows said, 'All that I am I give to you.' When I look back at that now, I see how wrong it was for me to have given 'all that I am.' Isn't it 'what I am' that made me the person that Simon had first fallen in love with? In my marriage vows, I had promised to give myself up and that is exactly what I did.

I can see now that I should not have given all of myself, but I did. I had nothing left of myself. Here's how I see it now, and I believe this to be an important point, especially for women.

I believe that every person is supposed to take up their correct amount of 'space' in the world.

I think this means emotional space; space to hold your own feelings, thoughts and opinions; space to blossom and grow and offer up to the world the joy of the unique abilities you bring to the universe; and space to just *be* the special and individual person that you are.

The single worst mistake I made in my life is that when I was in a codependent relationship, I was just *not taking up my allocated amount of space.*

At that time, I was giving up some of my quota of space in the world to Simon, so he ended up using more than his fair share of space. I was allowing him to blossom and grow, allowing him to hold his feelings as his and mine, and taking on his opinions as mine. My lesson from this is to never let someone else use space in this world that is allocated to me. This can happen in a marriage, at work, or in a family relationship, and it can happen easily if you let it.

It is important to note that I don't want to take any more space than is mine, and I don't want to take someone else's space off them; but I will never, ever give away any of my own space again. I intend to use just my exact amount of space, no more, no less.

The following analogy is the way that a healthy marriage (or relationship) has been best described to me:

Each individual needs to *build his or her own cake of life.* Each person needs to find his or her own career path, hobbies, friends, pastimes, and most importantly, values. So, my life cake may be chocolate with great big layers of chocolate ganache and grated dark chocolate shavings sprinkled over the top. My partner's cake may be a carrot cake with layers of cream cheese and drizzled with a nice maple syrup.

Now, here is the important bit. Your partner should not try to change your idea of what your cake is. It's your cake—stick to it. He doesn't have to like your chocolate cake of life; he can just enjoy his carrot cake without taking away from your chocolate. And don't try to take away his enjoyment of his carrot cake either.

So, if you are each building your own cake, and you are happy with it, what do you have to offer each other? You have that little something extra that will enhance your cake-eating experience. You can offer each other the *cherry on top*. The cherry on top is your shared joys, shared experiences, and the *value add* you offer to each other's life experience.

Now do you see the importance of this analogy? Your cake is fine as it is. It tastes great, looks good, and is very satisfying. Your partner's cake is also looking fantastic, yummy, and delicious. By adding the cherry to the top of each other's cake, you are not expecting the other to change his or her choice of cake; you just enhance each other's cake-life. Our relationships should be the *cherry on top* of life.

Well, I have taken this analogy quite literally, and I'm happy to say that I now have my own cake. It's a great flavor, too.

As my recovery continued, I realized that my self-minimalization had damaged me so badly that I needed to start taking up some more of my space in the world, so I went back to the one thing I did really well—making cake.

I started making and decorating cakes at home. After setting up a simple website, I was soon fully booked out with cake orders every week.

On the 15th August, one day before my second sobriety birthday, I opened Canberra's first and finest cupcake emporium.

Not out of spite, but because it was a journey I needed to travel on my own, I did absolutely everything in relation to setting up the cupcake emporium on my own. It was only my name on the lease and my name on the bank accounts. I wanted to stand or fall in this new venture on my own. I had no idea where this journey would lead, but I knew the lesson here was to learn it on my own.

My initial vision was that I would probably get enough business that I could run this small café and bake and sell maybe a couple of dozen cupcakes a day.

Well, I was in for the ride of my life. The cupcake business took off.

Fourteen to sixteen-hour working days became a regular part of my life. And now I was no longer doing these kinds of hours for my family—I was doing them for my business. It was an enormous change for our family as I went from being the person who had done everything for them to the one who had to focus on this amazingly fast-growing beast that was my business. I walked, talked, and slept cupcakes.

As with many new businesses, it does actually take time to find your feet, but I did eventually find them, and I was able to get my work/ life balance back in place. Most importantly, they were my feet. I did make some mistakes, and I have had some success, but they were my mistakes, and it is my success.

I now employ lots of staff. We sell thousands of cupcakes and many, many cakes every week, and we were announced as national finalists for the Australian Small Business Champion Awards.

This lesson, to be myself and follow my dreams, has been the most physically difficult of all the lessons I have learnt. However, it has also bought me the most joy and changes to my life that I did not think possible. It has literally made me a different person from the one I was before I began.

My lesson from this is to know that Simon's cake is great, fantastic, and superb as an accounting firm. That is his cake. I should never take away from that, but I should *never have made his cake flavour into my cake flavour.* I should have always built my own cake, and while we both built his cake, my cake went stale.

So go out, find your favourite cake flavour, and stick to it—because life *can* be lived without cake, but is it worthwhile?

Charm 14:

Standing in your own sunshine causes most of the shadows of your life.

Chapter 15

The Dunny
out the Back

(Self-Esteem)

My low self-esteem is at an all-time high.
—*Shia LaBeouf,* Transformers 2

With the opening of the cupcake emporium and the huge lessons that it had begun to teach me on being myself, I began to see changes in something that I thought was unsaveable: my self-esteem.

I was starting to think of myself as a *self*, which I had not felt for a very, very long time. My self-esteem had been at an all-time low on the day I entered detox, and now I was starting to get a little sense of what good self-esteem could be like to live with.

I don't think anyone is born with low self-esteem; I think the experiences of childhood and young adulthood often change our own opinion of ourselves.

I think that when we are born, we all think we are just right. Which is exactly what we are supposed to think. Good self-esteem is when you know that you are exactly what you are supposed to be right now. Not what you were, and not how you would be after the changes you would like to make to yourself; just how you are right now.

It does not mean that you don't think there are things you can work on, because hopefully we all think there are things that we can work on; but all the same, you are exactly the way you are supposed to be *right now*.

I used to have pretty good self-esteem in my teenage years. I think my mum did a pretty good job of making my siblings and me feel like we were exactly like we should have been. Not that I thought I was going to stay poor and uneducated forever or anything, but I knew that it was up to me to make something of myself, and I knew that I had that in me to do something as the years went on. I do remember knowing that other people had more money than us, but I also knew that I could get money if I worked hard enough, so I don't think that I thought they were any better than I was.

Anyway, I think it all went pear-shaped when I started thinking that I had to be something different from what I was. I began to think that in order to be loved by someone, I needed to be different from what I was. I think that is when my value in myself, my self-esteem, began to be badly affected.

As I got more and more into my relationship, I was so committed to keeping my marriage together that I was willing to change everything about myself in order to be what I thought my husband wanted, because in relatively short order, it did not appear that he was happy with what he had married.

I think that is where my self-esteem began to have a problem, because I was trying to be something I was not. I was quite happy with the *real* me, but then I started to try to be something I was not. I was not happy with the new me, and so my self-esteem went south.

As I became disappointed in myself, I self-medicated my anxieties by drinking to dissipate my feelings. Then the cycle began: bad self-esteem, drink to cover the bad self-esteem, feel worse, drink some more, and so it went on.

And so here I was now, in the midst of these changes in how I felt about myself and my value in the world, with the freedom to run my business and my life the way I saw fit. I started to realise that there was no way I was going to please everyone (staff and customers) and that sometimes I would have to believe in myself and make judgment calls based on my own values, not someone else's. Sometimes, this would disappoint other people, and they didn't mind telling me so. I was past the point of pleasing everyone, because one thing I have learnt about self-esteem is that the most important part of getting it right is in that first word, *self*.

You *cannot* get good self-esteem by attempting to change other people's opinions of you. That is an important point to remember that I had been missing for years and years.

What other people think of you is irrelevant to your self-esteem. You can spend your life doing everything that everyone else thinks is important; you can spend your life trying to look good, and be good, for everyone else; *but* if you are doing something (like drinking too much, in my case) that goes against your key values and you *know* deep down that this is not your *honest self,* then you will never, ever have good self-esteem.

I will never forget one day when I saw Dr Phil interviewing an alcoholic in the midst of her addiction. He was interviewing her and her family, who were essentially doing an intervention with her (on international TV). At one stage, Dr Phil called her up on something contradictory that she had just said. Her response was, 'I'm sorry, Dr Phil, but I really don't like you, so . . .' and she went on to say why she disagreed with him.

It was a light bulb moment for me when Dr Phil responded, 'Well, it is lucky, then, that my self-worth is in no way tied up in *your* opinion of me.' Wow! Did you hear the gravity of what he said? He had said that his esteem (value) of himself was not in any way connected to *her* opinion of him. This was a revelation to me. At that stage, I was still trying to *people-please* and therefore valued myself based on other people's opinion of myself.

Nowadays, my self-esteem is based on exactly that, *my* esteem (value) of myself. No-one else. Now, I would like to add that I do not go around intentionally hurting anyone, and I generally try to be a 'good' person. However, what I have learnt is that no matter what you do, or how hard you try, there will always, always be people who disagree with you, are upset by you, and do not actually like you. The important thing to remember is that *their* opinion of you should not reflect *your* opinion of you.

Women who have low self-esteem tend to think that everyone should be able to see how worthless they are. They expect to be treated as worthless (or close to it, depending on how far down the self-esteem scale they have gone). Mostly, the women will keep working and trying to change themselves to be what other people want in the deluded opinion that their self-esteem will get better when people think more of them.

I remember years ago when I first heard Oprah say you need to 'love yourself'. I am a big fan of Oprah's, love her work, but I thought, *What the hell? What is she talking about? What is the point in loving yourself? What does that even mean, anyway?*

But now I get it, because it means you need to love the place you are in *right now*. Forget next week, when you get a new job; or next month, when you lose a few pounds; or tomorrow, when you get into a loving relationship. Focus on right now!

Now, with me, like most addicts, when I was at my lowest, I just had plain old, easy-to-spot, low self-esteem. I think when most people looked at me, after a while they could see that I had low self-esteem. I did not come across as someone who was sure of herself or secure in her place in the world. Mine was the garden-variety low self-esteem, pretty much like most women who suffer low self-esteem.

Now, I'll let you in on a secret. There is a different kind of low self-esteem, which is a bit harder to spot, and it is *very often* found in the men who have low self-esteem. Here is the way I heard this kind of low self-esteem described:

An ego the size of a mansion *at the front, but the self-esteem the shape of the* dunny *out the back.*

In order to get your head around this, I like to put it this way:

Self-esteem is what you think of yourself, and the ego is what *you think* other people *should* think of you.

Now, from my experience, here is what many men with low self-esteem do.

They take their low self-esteem (like the dunny they actually think it is) and keep it hidden behind that great big ego mansion out the front. And guess what? They can't build that great big mansion out the front without help from other people, so they need *a lot* of ego-stroking to help keep that mansion on its foundations. These are the people who are so busy showing you how fabulous they want to be on the outside so that even they can ignore their dunny out the back.

One of the hardest problems is to live with or love one of the people in the second category. These people will rely on the people around them to keep their mansions up. They will surround themselves with yes-men and people-pleasers, and of course, a good co-dependent spouse is always a really good bonus. It is very, very hard work to be around these people. They cannot even be seen to be keeping their mansions up, as then they would have to admit the truth to themselves—that they need to have you around them holding the mansion up and standing between them and their dunny, ever protecting them from the horrible truth that they don't actually love themselves either. It is very, very hard work, and of course is an unachievable goal because whether this person is your spouse, your child, or your boss, it is *not your job* to keep that person's mansion up.

If you are in low self-esteem category 2, then you first need to strip away your ego, knock down your mansion, find your dunny, and then read some books and learn how to love yourself!!

If you are in low self-esteem category 1, then you need to do some reading to learn how to love yourself. Learn to love *yourself* right now, for who you are right now. The journey to good self-esteem is long, but worthwhile. You can incorporate many of the other lessons from your journey into your toolkit for good self-esteem.

You owe it to yourself to build your self-esteem to exactly where it should be for you to live the best life you can live. You can only be, and do, in this world what you were put here to do, if you know that *you* were the only person put here to do it.

To live with low self-esteem is such hard work and so painful that it is easy to wonder why you are here at all. My journey to good self-esteem has actually been one of the easiest to learn. This is because so many of the other lessons have helped me realise the importance of my own value and I have incorporated so much of this wisdom to build my self-esteem. It is a beautiful thing to know that you, and you alone, have the power to build your self-esteem for happiness and the best life you can live, as I have done.

Charm 15:

The important word in 'self-esteem' is self. You, and only you, have the power to build your best self.

Chapter 16

I'm Only Lonely
When I'm Around

(Alone vs Lonely)

You cannot be lonely if you like the person you are alone with.

—Wayne Dyer

There is no hiding the fact that our society is geared towards us all doing things in pairs.

To travel as a single guest, you pay the same for a room as a double, and every table in every restaurant is set for two, not for one.

Let alone so much of what our society believes to be 'right' is based on the Cinderella syndrome. This is our society's belief that our lives only begin when we have found the man of our dreams, and so we can, you guessed it, live happily ever after.

This was absolutely my belief when I was a young adult. I was definitely of the understanding that I needed to do things in a particular order. First, I needed to get engaged and then married, buy a house of our own, followed closely by starting a family, and then on to buy/start a business. The rest would be history.

And as I was such a stickler for control, this is, of course, just what I did. And Simon and I would go on to spend twenty-four/seven together for many, many years in order to make this plan happen.

So if, on the day I was taken into detox, someone had told me that there was a risk of separating from my husband after I got sober, I one hundred percent would not have chosen to go into that detox. Staying married was part of my being; it was the essence of who I was, and at that stage, I was in fact not a whole human being without Simon. I would have chosen death before divorce.

So it is an understatement to say how astounding it was that less than three years into sobriety, I was finally ready to admit that Simon and I could no longer save our marriage. To our credit, right up until the day we decided to separate, we had still always thought we could work it out and stay together. We never *settled* for a bad marriage; we just always thought that we could work it out.

For the last year of the marriage, there had been constant feelings of tension among everyone in the family, and Simon and I had been attending counseling together to work on the codependency-based issues that were the root of our problems. Simon and I did fight quite regularly; I mean, I was literally changing before his eyes. You do not have the kind of emotional growth that I had had without it affecting the relationships you are in. If any of our friends or family knew what was going on, it was once again the 'elephant in the room' that was not discussed. It is a human condition that we all like to think that our friends and loved ones are tracking on okay, and we don't really want to see that they are in pain. So no one really talked about it, just assuming, I think, that since I had sobered up, then everything was going to be okay from here on in.

I had been in so much pain up until this time. I really did feel unloved by Simon, and perhaps he by me. I am not really sure now where love ever sat within our relationship. Perhaps we were always too focused on the end goal of success; I don't think we ever stopped to smell the roses. I wanted the pain to stop. I wanted to be loved and to love someone. And when push came to shove, Simon and I really did not have anything in common anymore. If we had met at a party as newly single people at that time, we would not have chatted more than a second. There was no spark, no connection. All we had left by that time was history, and it was very painful history. I know some people will say that if you work hard enough at it, you can get the spark back; but I think we really tried, and in the end, we could not.

We were both at the stage where we had put absolutely everything into trying to save the marriage. My way of describing our marriage by that time was to say that we had painted the marriage every colour in the rainbow, but it was still not rosy. Simon's description was that every shred of flesh had been pulled from the bones of our marriage. Both are probably true analogies.

The saddest and most difficult thing either of us has ever done was to decide to break up our family unit. It is heart-wrenching and painful. No one can prepare you for it, even if, like in my situation, both parties understand that they must move forward. Of course I wish that I could have prevented putting my children through the pain of a divorce, and God knows I tried.

And so, Simon and I had what was a very 'amicable' divorce, and it still hurt like hell. It is still a grieving process, and if there was one thing I had learnt on my journey, it was the importance of feeling those feelings, and so I allowed the whole grieving process to work its way through me.

Simon stayed in the family home, I moved to a house within a few suburbs, and we agreed on equal custody of the children. We tried to keep the children's life as stable as possible, as they were able to stay in the same school and just spent half the week with me and half with Simon.

But the exciting part of this journey was that for the first time in many, many years, I had a couple of days each week to spend on my own.

I remember the first week of our separation, when it was the first night that Simon would have the kids. I hadn't thought that much about it before that, but as I was leaving work, one of my staff members asked casually, 'What are you doing tonight?'

And suddenly it hit me like a lightning bolt that for the first time in about twenty years, I could do whatever I wanted, eat whatever I wanted, and go wherever I wanted!

What a gift—the joy of spending time alone! I cannot tell you how exciting this was for me. I was not scared of being alone, and I think all the work I had done on my self-esteem is to thank for that. I was forty-one, fabulous, and free to do whatever I wanted.

And so the question becomes, when does being alone become lonely? I think the answer to this is that when being alone makes you sad, then you are lonely.

I believe there are some very important reasons for spending time alone and some excellent reasons why this should not mean you are lonely.

Firstly, time spent alone is a key element in the journey of emotional growth. Remember, if you do not grow to become a worthwhile, substantial human being all on your own, then you will only ever be that one half of the Velcro.

Time spent alone will allow you to develop your own values and truths, teach you to know what is important in your life, and help make you the person that you are meant to be.

Secondly, if you do not spend time alone, you will literally become a boring person. If every experience (or a large chunk of them) is spent with another person, you will just not have enough independent experiences in your life to make you interesting. A key point to remember when you are deciding how much fun another person is to be with is to think the same of yourself: *Would I date or spend time with me?* If the answer is *No, all I ever talk about is my kids or my husband or my significant other and all of their activities,* then probably you wouldn't want to spend time with you, so why would anyone else?

Another important reason to spend time on your own is to make sure that you are not *afraid* to spend time alone. I have spoken to many, many women who have stayed in bad or unhappy marriages because they have convinced themselves that it is better than being alone. If you are well practiced at spending time alone within a relationship, then you will never be afraid to be alone, and then you will not stay in a relationship to prevent loneliness. I am a big believer that we should only stay in a relationship if it is good for both people involved, not because we are fearful of what it would be like outside of the relationship.

Some of the things I love to do when I am spending time on my own include:

1. **Going to the movies.** Yes, you can do this alone. I have a friend who comes from a small town who used to tell me that when she was a kid, the old crazy woman in the village was the one who went to the movies on her own, and so all these years later, she would still not go alone for fear of being known as the old crazy lady! Well, perhaps we all think like this and we really don't feel comfortable sitting on our own at the movies. But once you get used to it, you will lose your fear of buying a ticket for one, and you will love the emotional growth that comes from enjoying a movie on your own.

2. **Exercising.** Whilst exercising as part of a group is great, it is also a fabulous growth experience to know the joys of exercising on your own. A walk around the lake, along the beach, or in your local national park is unsurpassed as an experience that can heal your spirit.

3. **Learning a new skill.** Whilst this often involves being part of a class environment, it is also great to also learn something different from your significant other or your children. There are an unlimited number of classes available at your local TAFE, both during the day and at night, and they are normally very affordable.

4. **Traveling alone.** Now, I have spoken to some people who believe this idea is absolutely unthinkable, so I *dare* you to do it! I know it means that you will be paying for a room that two people can stay in, but believe me, it is well worthwhile. Now, I am the first to tell you that

going on holiday with someone that you love and enjoy the company of is fantastic and can hardly be beaten, *but* if you think hard enough, you will find a place and a time that your significant other or your children are not that keen on. Use this as a reason to go there yourself! The growth you will develop by travelling in challenging environments on your own is unequalled.

Always remember that time spent alone should be a life-giving experience. Too much time alone spent on Facebook, shopping online, computer games, or anything similar to this is not going to add to your emotional growth.

I would like to offer an important point of caution on the tale of 'alone versus lonely'. Too much time on your own is also not good for you! Some people, particularly people in the midst of some type of addiction or depressive behaviour, can tend to isolate themselves so they can avoid the growth lessons that life in the real world and relationships with other people can offer them.

If you are isolating yourself, you will know it. Don't do it. Like everything in life, do it in moderation and from a healthy intention.

Spending time on your own to learn to know yourself will make you a better person for other people to be around, and a better person to be alone with.

So as I worked my way through my third year of sobriety, I did it with a freedom I had never known. I was lucky enough to build a balance between decreased working hours in my cupcake emporium and a home life full of joy. When I had Josie and Jackson with me, we had many fun times where the three of us enjoyed shared activities. I enjoyed spending time on my own, either going to movies or travelling solo, and lots of nice quiet time in a house of my own. I went forward as a fearless woman full of hope for an *uncharted* future for the first time in my life.

Charm 16:

You are only alone when you don't know yourself.

Chapter 17

The Committee in Your Head

(Thoughts)

Our life is what our thoughts make it.
—Marcus Aurelius

There is nothing more powerful than the thoughts in our heads.

It is a well-used sales strategy to make customers believe that they have thought of an idea to buy this product on their own, because if they thought of it themselves, then it must be true. We all believe ourselves.

If you are a wife, you may have used this strategy yourself. You have a job that needs doing around the house, and you know your hubby is really not going to be that interested in getting it done. So you get him to believe that it is his idea, and he will do it for sure!

We all believe the thoughts in our head are true.

I had more than two years of sobriety under my belt and quite a lot of lessons learned by this time, but this one caught me by surprise. It was another interesting paradox for me that during my drinking years and early in my sobriety, I didn't even think I listened to what was in my head at all. I thought I just listened to everyone else, did what they said, and thought what they thought. In essence, subjugating my ideas and thoughts was also a big part of my codependency.

However, I *had* actually been listening to the thoughts in my head. I had been listening to all the rubbish I had been telling me about what I *could not* do, what I had *done wrong,* and how much more I *had to do.* Negative self-talk. And I totally believed all of the stuff that my mind was telling me. Why wouldn't I? It was me talking, after all. Even in early sobriety, when I actually had a lot to congratulate myself on (like surviving another day without picking up a drink), I still had a head full of negative talk, and it affected the way I thought about myself.

It was a confronting day when I learned that our heads do not tell us the *truth* all the time. It happened to me at this time because my self-esteem was starting to flourish and some of the usual thoughts that were bouncing around in my mind did not gel any longer with my reality.

Anne and I had met up again at our usual haunt, and not surprisingly, in her wisdom, she had the clue to what was going on for me. 'Sharon, the thoughts in our heads only have the ability to see life through the filters that life has given us. Our thoughts are based on our upbringing and, in your case, your experiences. You have had such negative self-talk for the majority of your life, some of which may have been true back in its day, but it is no longer true.' She went on to say, 'You need to start doing two things. One is to stop believing everything your head is telling you as a truth, and secondly, replace the negative self-talk with positive.'

This was a revelation to me, and I was excited that once again I was being shown how I alone had the power to change this. The negative self-talk had been the trigger for so many of my more painful emotions, and here I was being told that I had the power to rid myself of this pain.

What an exciting concept! Positive change was afoot. As usual, I started reading about this concept and went on to make changes in my behaviours. This time, I had no one else to practice on but me, because this was all about changes in my own mind.

In many ways, it is as simple as this. It's all about allowing incorrect thoughts into your mind and allowing them to become truths. If you were brought up in a family where you were told that you were rubbish, lowly, and worthless, then in the end, your head would still be telling you that you are rubbish, lowly, and worthless, and you *would* believe it.

If, however, you were brought up by parents who told you that you had unique abilities and you could achieve anything, then this is exactly what your mind will believe to be true.

So here is where the key to change lies: You do not have to believe what your head tells you. You need to understand that the information being sent to you is coming through a filter and it changes the message that is sent to you.

Imagine that you have had a horrific day. You were late to work, you were unable to get the project your boss had allocated you for the day, and you lost a big customer for the company because of it. You are on your way home, and you walk past a friend of yours; you raise your hand to wave, and she walks past as if to ignore you. Your mind says, *Oh, crap, Susie is snubbing me. I'd snub me too. I'm a crap employee, crap friend, and totally worthless.*

However, what if your day had started differently? You were fresh, alert, and on time. Your boss gave you the project, and you absolutely nailed it. You won over the new customer, and they signed up for a big contract. You are walking home, feeling on top of the world, when you notice Susie walking past. You raise your hand to wave, and she does not respond. *Oh, Susie is obviously deep in thought, so she didn't see me. I hope she has had an okay day. I'll give her a call later tonight and say hi because our friendship is important.*

This story highlights the importance of not acting on our thoughts before deciding on how true they are. If the girl in this story had responded in the first scenario by getting angry or upset at her friend Susie, then she could have ruined their friendship.

These situations occur often in everyday life. Many of the relationships in our lives would be different if we had not acted immediately on the thoughts we were being told at the time.

Thoughts are not facts; they are filtered.

An important point to remember when you are listening to what your head says to you: If in doubt, *don't*.

You can just watch your thoughts come and go. You do not have to act on them, and they are not always the truth.

Generally speaking, it is not going to do any harm to wait and see if your head tells you something different once your mood, or your filter on the situation, has changed. It is only in times of immediate, life-threatening danger that an immediate response is required. So, in most cases, just wait and see what the committee in your head tells you later. The outcome can be very different, and mostly for the better.

Another thing that we allow our minds to do is to over-think things. Strangely, we are of the opinion that if we think, think, think about things, we can change the response of another person, and therefore we can change the outcome. We do not have the power to change another person's response. We cannot change it by over-thinking it.

Have you ever played out a whole conversation in your head before it happens? You decide who's right, who's wrong, what they will say, what you will say in response, and so it goes on. Those conversations are *so* painful and such a waste of time. By having these conversations, you are allowing someone to live in your head, rent-free.

By remembering that we have no control over another person's response, we can know that all we need to do in these situations is to do and say 'the next right thing' and leave the outcome to God. We have no control over outcomes. Our control stops at the end of our noses.

Let it go. Just *let it go*.

We can often make the mistake of over-thinking something that has happened in the past too. Thinking about something that has happened to you or something someone has done to you, cannot, I repeat, absolutely cannot, change what has happened. It does not matter how bad it was or how unfair you think it is; you still can't change it. You also can't make them pay for what they have done by thinking about it. You cannot make them remorseful, and you cannot make them sorry.

It was timely that I had begun to learn this lesson early in my separation from Simon. Even though our separation was completely by mutual agreement because we both knew without a shadow of a doubt that we needed to move on, I was still deeply in grief for the loss of our family unit. During this time, Janine asked why I was still angry with Simon when we had both agreed to separate. I said to her that I was angry that our relationship had died the 'death of a thousand cuts', and each of those cuts for me was a time that Simon had hurt me over the years.

'What do you want him to do about that now to stop you being angry?' she asked.

As I had over-thought this so much, I responded, 'I want him to pick up the phone and apologise to me every day of his life until I ask him to stop.' I wanted him to feel some of the pain that I felt, even though I knew by then that you cannot control how another person feels.

I have heard this lesson best taught by Oprah when she said, 'This is like drinking the poison yourself and expecting the other person to die.'

I was very grateful when I started to learn this lesson on the power of thoughts. Six months after my separation, I had a moment of clear and immediate realization. It didn't matter that Simon had not felt my pain, and it did not matter that he would never again say he was sorry to me; what mattered was that I was in control of how I felt. Simon was not, and never had been, in control of how I felt. It was all up to me to feel my feelings, so I just *let it go*. Petrea King, a well-regarded expert on grief counseling, says that when we come to a place in our lives that we realize that when *we want peace more than we want to be right*, then we will move on.

And so I did.

Another mistake we often make is to over-think what *other people* think of us. We can all spend a lot of time making sure that people think highly of how we look, what we do, what we say, and how we act. But it is such a waste of time to spend your emotional and physical energy on worrying what other people think of us, because we have no control over what other people think of us. *It is none of your business what another person thinks of you.*

This lesson is a simple lesson to hear but a very difficult lesson to incorporate into our lives. Obviously, this lesson links quite closely to the lesson on perfection (because you will never do everything to keep everyone happy) and self-esteem (because you have to be nice and comfortable with yourself).

Each of us should live our lives true to our own values and ideals, without the intention of hurting another person but without changing ourselves only to please the people around us. This is one of the key elements of a fulfilling and worthwhile life, so it is an important lesson to incorporate into our lives.

One of the many things that surprised me as I started changing my behaviours to reflect this lesson is that I was *so* used to trying to change myself to make everyone else happy that it actually *felt wrong* to be doing what was true to myself. I felt guilty for having my own truths and values and for not living by someone else's. And I hate guilt. It has always been one of the hardest feelings I have had to learn to 'sit' with. Of course, thinking logically, I knew that I had no reason to be guilty, as all I was doing was living my own life; but as it was such a new experience for me, I had to sit with that feeling of guilt and wrongness for quite a while before it started to feel normal to live life with my own ideals and not someone else's. So, as with all lessons, the trick for me was to practice and to continue to sit with all these new feelings that my new positive thoughts and behaviours brought about.

There is one final point I would like to make about the power of positive thinking.

There are two schools of thought on this matter that I think are owed consideration. The first is the 'fake it till you make it' theory. This has been used in therapy for a number of years. It essentially means, in regard to this lesson, that if we think positively, we feel positive, and then we are positive. We can incorporate this type of thinking into all areas of our lives, and although if you are used to thinking negatively, it does take a while to make this a normal behaviour pattern, I feel it is well worth the work.

The second school of thought is that our thoughts are a form of energy, and basically, if we send positive energy (thoughts) out to the universe, then we will get positive energy right back again.

There is lots of reading to be done in this area if you would like to learn how to change your thought patterns to lead to a more positive life, but one thing is for sure: it can't do you any harm, so why not give it a go?

Go forward in your journey with the knowledge that your thoughts do not rule you, and they are not always telling you the truth. You may not be able to control what the committee in your head says to you, but you can control what you listen to.

Charm 17:

Our thoughts do not always *tell us* the truth.

Chapter 18
News Flash!

(Control)

You can't always control the wind, but you can always control your sails.
—Anthony Robbins

One year to the day after our separation, Simon and I had an appointment to see our divorce lawyer. We had always been all-or-nothing kind of people, and it was not that either of us was dying to get married to someone else or anything; we just wanted to be either married or divorced. Separated was a kind of limbo that neither of us liked. By law, we had to be separated for a year and a day, so we were unable to do it any sooner than this, but we were not going to take any longer either.

I was feeling free and in charge of my own destiny.

What I was soon to learn is that we are never in charge of our whole destiny. We are only in charge of our reactions to the things that are destined to happen.

I had lived so many years trying to control everything that was not mine to control. I had been trying to control everyone else's feelings, thoughts, and life journeys. In the old days, I did not know how to live without control; I was using it as mechanism to manage my anxieties. Since then, I had learnt that I was trying to control the madness that was my life. I did not mean to control anyone around me; I just tried to control all the circumstances around me to prevent anything going wrong. During my period of recovery, I had learnt that I could not manage my anxieties by trying to control other people, but I did not realise that there were many *outcomes* I could not control either.

Well, when Simon and I separated and then got divorced, I had a very big lesson in letting go of the outcomes.

Before I moved out of the house, we had sent out a joint email to all our friends telling everyone about our separation. We were clear about the facts that it was an amicable separation and that we would be co-parenting Josie and Jackson.

I had thought that because we had known most of our friends for many years—since at least when our children were young, if not before—we would carry on as friends. Simon and I were happy to get invited to the same events and functions, as we were comfortable being in the same room together, even once we each started dating other people.

However, that is not how it panned out.

Apparently (I've been told since this time), people really struggle with a divorce situation without seeing one person in the right and the other person in the wrong. It is a human condition to want to have someone to blame.

So, for many of the people we knew, I became the person to blame.

At first, I just noticed that I was dropped off some email lists and not invited to some of the parties. But then it started to get nasty. I started to hear gossip, for want of a better word, about things that I had apparently done or said to Simon which were completely untrue. Things began to get hurtful. I don't believe, for the most part, that these rumours were started by Simon, and that is not what I am trying to imply. The issue here was that essentially, people had nothing bad to say about me, so they made it up.

And over this, I had no control.

I watched as the gossip got worse and worse, more hurtful every time. At its peak, the innuendo made its way not only to my personal Facebook wall, but also onto the cupcake emporium Facebook page, which affected not only me but my staff and my customers. I felt like a D-list celebrity with the sordid untruths of my divorce plastered over the pages of the entertainment news.

During this period, I spoke at length to Anne. I was in a great deal of pain. I knew that until now, my control issues had been related to my over-functioning and to my codependency. However, now this control issue was about other people and what they were doing and saying about me. Anne said, 'Sharon, each action you take is the right one based on your own truths and values. It cannot be based on what other people are going to think about you. You can see now that you must be brave in this endeavour, as it is difficult, and it does test your faith in yourself and your own values.'

And right then, I had, as Oprah would say, an ah-ha moment. There is only one single thing in this whole world that I can control:

I—can—only—control—*me*. Full stop.

I cannot control what *happens* to me; I can only control how I *respond* to those events. So, if you are like me and you are trying to control the *people, places, and things* around you, then you might as well stop it now because it is a *great big waste of time and energy.*

I will not pretend to you that this is a lesson that can be easily let go of, even when it comes in a lightning-bolt moment like this. I have to work on this issue every single day, and I am often reminded of this quote, which is a version of the serenity prayer that helps me to remember:

> God grant me the serenity to accept the people I cannot change,
> the courage to change the one I can,
> and the wisdom to know it's me.

This prayer is very insightful when you think about it. It actually has the key to many of our emotional issues all wrapped up in one sentence.

And so, in this situation where I was being misrepresented and gossiped about unfairly, the best thing I could do was to *let it go*.

I did not respond, and I did not lower myself to the level of those people who had been causing me this pain. I did not allow these people any 'rent-free space in my head' while I worried about what they, or anyone else, thought about me. I decided that anyone who believed these untruths was not someone I would like as my friend anyway. In these choices to *let it go,* I found peace in an otherwise stressful and hurtful situation.

I cannot impress upon you strongly enough how important it is to learn the lesson on giving up control. You will find your world will change. I have found that so many of the other lessons are incorporated in this lesson. You will feel that such a weight has been lifted from you because in the end, it is such a fantastic relief to not have to try to control the outcomes of the world anymore. It was so exhausting.

To live without control in your life is to live with the stresses of the world whizzing around you, but not affecting your own happiness. You no longer need to buy into what people think of you; you cannot control that. You no longer need to worry about how you will fix everything; it is not yours to fix. You no longer need to predict what will happen in the future; it is not your job to make it happen. You no longer need to question what happens; the answer is not yours to give. The biggest, most heart-wrenching problems down to the smallest, most trivial of dilemmas can all be handed over. Each time you are given a decision, just do the next best thing and leave the outcome to the universe. *Just let it go.*

So, always remember that your control stops right at the end of your nose.

As I moved away from this painful time in my life, I had finally given up the last droplet of control I thought I had over the uncontrollable river of life. I did, however, learn I had control to choose which life-raft I would jump onto in order to travel smoothly through the rest of my journey.

Charm 18:

Letting go of control will feel like the end of the world, but it is the beginning of a new life.

Chapter 19
Do Not Reinvent the Wheel

(Wisdom)

I'm not young enough to know everything.
—J.M. Barrie

Sharon Mitchell

So here I was, living joyously through my third year of sobriety with more freedom, peace, happiness, and blessings than I had ever enjoyed in my life.

I thought back to my early days of sobriety, when Anne had said to me that it would take three to five years before I started to feel the real benefits of recovery. As usual, she had been right. At the time, though, I had been quite grumpy at the prospect of waiting so long to feel better, and I just didn't understand why I could not work it out right then and right there. Of course, the answer is twofold. First, you need to find the right person, or book with information that is right for you; and secondly, you need to practice. Both of these things take time.

But of course, the most important thing was that I needed to be open to learning new lessons to gain wisdom.

This had been the new concept for me because when I was a young adult, I thought *without a doubt* that I knew everything.

When I met a person who was divorced, I thought they had just made the wrong decisions in their marriage and not worked hard enough. I thought I knew better.

When I met a person who claimed not to need money to be happy, I would think that the person was just making that excuse because he or she had not made enough money, and I could make more.

When I met someone who had children who were, I thought, out of control, I would assume that I could be stricter and tougher and I could raise children better.

My sixteen-year old-son recently described eloquently how most of us felt as young people: 'Mum, I don't think I know everything. I *know* I know everything.'

The paradox of gaining wisdom is that the wiser you get, the more you realize what you *don't* know.

The best philosophical definition of wisdom that I have heard is this: *Wisdom is the ability to understand events and act on them to consistently produce optimum results with the least amount of negative energy.*

To me, this means, very simply, that *we should learn from our mistakes.* This is why another common definition for wisdom is to *celebrate our mistakes,* because we cannot gain wisdom without making mistakes.

The problem for me is that for much of my adult life, I was not learning from my mistakes.

My life had become like *Groundhog Day,* a 1993 movie where the main character wakes up every day to the same day. It was the same day of his life, just repeated over and over, day after day. That is kind of what my life was. I would live my life, God would show me lessons, and I would ignore them and gain no wisdom. Then I would wake up the next day and make the same mistakes again and again. The definition of insanity is to repeat the same behaviours and expect a different outcome, but this is exactly what I was doing. If someone had said to me in the days before my recovery that I had no wisdom during my adult years, I would have been angry.

I thought that since I was married, had children, and ran a business, then I obviously had learned something, and therefore I had wisdom.

However, although I had learned many practical tasks, like how to make money, change nappies, and hire and fire staff, I had not actually taken any notice of the important stuff, *like emotional maturity.* I had learned how to make a living, but not a *life.*

I am very, very grateful that my rock bottom was so horrific and left me so close to death. It meant that when I began my journey into recovery, I was so deflated and so broken that right from the beginning, I was ready to admit that everything I had ever held as true until that time must be complete rubbish.

I had gone from a position of knowing that I knew everything to a position of knowing that I actually knew nothing.

This was perhaps the biggest blessing I have ever been given.

I very quickly learned that as far as recovery goes, the best thing to do is to find people who have already done it well and follow their guidance. It's actually that easy.

The day I met Anne was such a blessing for me, as I had just come to this realization, the awareness that I actually knew very little, and nothing of any value at all when it came to emotional growth. Anne was quick to point out to me that there was no point in her sharing her thoughts with me through this journey if I was not in a position where I was ready to learn. She said she would be asking me to feel feelings and address things from my past that would be painful and full of hurt. She said I would not understand many things that she said to me (which I didn't), but when the time was right for me to understand that lesson, I would learn (which I did).

I started my journey with Anne as an apprentice to the master, Anne showing me each of the tools of life and explaining how to use it. I have learnt how to use so many of the tools from the toolkit of life that were given to me, so we are now good friends still progressing further through our journey together. What was once daily contact in order to keep my sanity through my dark periods has become joyous and fun-filled dinner parties with our family and friends.

Many times over these years, people have asked me what the key to my recovery is, and I have always responded, 'All I ever did was find someone wiser than me and listen to her. That is the answer to all the questions.'

The easiest way to wisdom is to *not* reinvent the wheel.

No matter what area of your life that you look into, you will find someone who has already done it, and most of the time, that person will be happy to share his or her knowledge with you.

The problem with most of us younger people is that we do not *ask* those people wiser than us for help. Guess what (and this is a big pebble, so listen up)—*wise people will not offer advice unsolicited;* however, *unwise people give it freely.*

For example, I have sat in many, many rooms now with people who have less sobriety and less recovery from alcoholism than me, and I *never* offer advice unless they ask me for it.

The reason some wise people never offer unsolicited advice is that they *know* that a teacher cannot teach until the pupil is ready to learn. You will not hear the lesson unless you are ready to learn that lesson. There is absolutely no point in me sharing any of my lessons on how to get and keep good sobriety until someone sitting in that room is ready to hear it, so I don't.

So, if you want to prevent yourself from living in *Groundhog Day,* then learn from the wise people.

Now here comes the word of caution on this matter. Not everyone who thinks they are wise on a particular subject *is* wise on a particular subject.

So how do we decide whom we should listen to and whom we should ignore?

My answer is that is to find people who are doing what they are doing well and ask them what works for them. So, if you are looking for advice on how to improve your relationship, then find a person whom you believe is happy and ask him or her about it. If you are looking to improve your work life, find someone who is doing really well in business and ask what works for him or her. If you are looking for a spiritual awakening or emotional growth, then look for a person who radiates serenity and ask how he or she does it.

Remember, these people are likely to be quiet achievers. They are not likely to be the people at a party who are loudly sharing how best to make your next million on the stock market. They are likely to be the happy, healthy ones speaking of the joys in their lives. I use this technique frequently now, and if I go to a party, I do not look for the 'cool kids' with their new Versace handbags, but I search out anyone who is sixty-plus and start quizzing them on their secret to happiness. When I was invited to a thirtieth birthday party recently, I was very excited when the host mentioned that her grandma was going to be there but would have no-one to talk to. 'Great!' I piped up. 'Please, put her next to me.' I walked away from that party wiser than I came in.

Finally, I would like to say that you need never follow anything anyone ever tells you and do it to the letter of the law. Sometimes, what they offer to you may work for you one hundred percent, and you can just take that little pebble of wisdom and slip it straight into your life. However, you may like to take the information, use what is relevant to you, and then throw the rest away.

Wisdom is like a recipe. Imagine that you gave the same recipe to five chefs and asked them to make that recipe for you. Each of the chefs would take the recipe and make it his or her own. They would all come back to you with their own dishes, and you would have five different dishes. Each dish would have the same key elements, but they would all be a little different in their own way.

Our lives, and the lessons we incorporate into our lives, are the same as these recipes. All of our journeys are different but good all the same, so search out your own wise chefs and make your own recipe for a happy life.

Charm 19:

You don't know what you don't know; listen to those who do.

Chapter 20

Life Is for the Livin'

(Enjoy)

Life is meant to be lived.

—*Eleanor Roosevelt*

As this amazing life sits before me, I head towards my fourth sobriety birthday. Things have happened in this journey that would have killed me just years beforehand. I have undertaken what is perhaps the most difficult journey this life has to offer: the journey of self-awareness.

I remember a day not long before I was released from the detox unit, before all this began, when I realized that towards the end of my drinking, my life had become a struggle for survival, not a life of challenges and achievements as it had once been.

I decided that I needed a plan. There was much excitement amongst the other residents of the unit about this because anything that did not involve a blood test or watching the small, grainy TV in the common room was reason for enthusiasm.

I sat in the common room and devised my plan of things that I thought I could achieve, if I worked hard for the rest of my life. At the time, I thought that these things were quite difficult challenges, so far from what I had been capable of in the time leading up to that. I left the detox unit thinking that if I could achieve this list before I died, I would be going well.

I completed everything on that list before I was six weeks sober! They are things that now seem trivial in comparison to what I now know I can now achieve.

Not long after this time, I was relaying this story to my friend William, an alcoholic with many years of sobriety. He said to me, 'Sharon, never put a cap on what you think you can achieve in your sobriety. It is never-ending.'

Of course he was right, and it is actually true for everyone. Before I had learnt the lessons that recovery has given me, I really had no idea what life could offer me. I thought 'perfect' was perfect business, perfect marriage, perfect kids, perfect house. I thought that was me, and I thought that was *enough,* and I thought that was all that I would ever do. I thought I was doing *perfectly.*

What I did not realize was that I was so busy trying to do my perfect life that I had pigeonholed myself into this life that was built on fear of failure, and I was stopping myself from even seeing the possibilities of all the other things I could achieve in life. I also thought that this was everything I would ever want. As was my pattern at that time, I saw everything in black and white, no grey and no room for growth or change.

I thought that what I thought then was what I would think *forever.* What I know now is that what is important to me now might not be important to me later down the track. I recently had a customer come into the cupcake emporium to show me her cupcake tattoo (we get them fairly regularly!). She was completely surprised to hear that I did not have a cupcake tattoo. 'Why not?' she asked.

I had to reply, 'Because this cupcake shop will be just one small part of my journey. I intend that there will be so many of these steps in my journey that I may not have the room for body-art of everything!'

Imagine there is a bank account that credits your account each morning with $86,400. But it does not keep any of your money until the next day. If there is any money that is left in the account that you did not use that day, it gets deleted by the bank each night. Would you spend every dollar? Yes, you would!

Every one of us has this bank. It is *time.*

Every morning, it credits you with 86,400 seconds.

Every night, it writes off as a loss whatever you have failed to invest to a good purpose. It doesn't carry over a balance. This bank does not allow an overdraft. Each day, it opens a new account for you. Each night, it destroys what is left.

If you fail to use the day's deposits, the loss is yours. There is no drawing against tomorrow.

You must live in the present on today's deposits. Invest it so as to get from it the utmost in health, happiness, and success. Make the most of today.

Start by making a list of the things that you would like to do, whom you would like to meet, where you would like to go. And don't be stingy! There is a lot of research to prove that people with written-down goals are more likely to achieve them. Whether you make it a written list or a vision board, go with whatever suits you, but make it *big!* Make great big visions for yourself to fill your life with events and people that will challenge you, and you will grow.

Do not allow yourself to suffer from the 'someday' syndrome. Get up and start your journey now, because *someday is here.*

So today, I jump out of bed feeling blessed every day to have been given the opportunity for this journey that has brought me to a place of health, happiness, and hope. I think Josie and Jackson have grown through this experience of having me, an alcoholic in recovery, as their mother. They are happy and healthy and getting up to all the right sorts of things that teenagers should be doing. I hope that I have been able to teach them just a few of the things I have learnt, but their journey is their own, and it will be a joy for me to watch them grow up through my sober eyes. I live my amends to them every day that I stay sober. I have a good relationship with my ex-husband, their father, and we continue to co-parent quite successfully. Our relationship is no longer based on the pain we caused each other or on our history as we grew and matured; it is now as friends who are both proud to share the last names of our children.

I am now also blessed to be in a very special relationship with a beautiful man whose spirit and passion for life make my journey even more fun. The love for my cupcakes and cakes and the business it has become has given me the courage to believe in myself, my dreams, my beliefs, and even my ability to share this story with you.

So, I have gone forward from my darkness of ignorance into the sunlight of awareness, through the wisdom and knowledge of others. I am never going to learn less. Life is there for me to go out and live, and I shall do it every single day.

So, if life really is a dance floor, do not stand watching from the balcony—go out and dance!

Charm 20:

Today is guaranteed; tomorrow isn't. Live today to the full.

Recommended Reading List

These books are just some of the books I have read during my journey, and I can recommend each one of them to you. I have noted my particular favourites with an asterisk (*). I found that these had very valuable lessons which led to turning points in my recovery.

Feelings:

1. *The Language of Feelings* (David Viscott, MD, Pocket Books)
2. *Feelings Buried Alive Never Die* (Karol K. Truman, Bringham Distributing)

Fear:

1. *Feel the Fear and Do It Anyway* (Susan Jeffers, PhD, Hay House)
2. *The Dance of Fear* (Harriet Learner, PhD, Harper Paperbacks) *
3. *Comfortable with Uncertainty* (Pema Chodron, Shambhala Publications)

Tolerance:

1. *Many Paths, One Destination* (Ram Ramakrishnan, Wheatmark)
2. *Why Men Don't Listen and Women Can't Read Maps* (Allan Pease, Three Rivers Press)
3. *The Art of Connecting* (Claire Raines and Lara Ewing, Amacon)

Emotional Growth:

1. *Quantum Wellness* (Kathy Freston, Doubleday) *
2. *Healthy Mind, Healthy Woman* (Alice D. Domar, PhD, Dell Publishing)
3. *I Thought It Was Just Me* (Brené Brown, PhD Gotham Books)

Addiction:

1. *Addict in the Family* (Beverly Conyers, Hazelden Publishing)
2. *The Enabler* (Angelyn Miller, MA, Wheatmark)
3. *I Am Your Disease* (Sheryl Letzgus-McGinnis, Outskirts Press)

Truth:

1. *Understanding Other People* (Beverly D. Flaxington, ATA Press)
2. *Everyday Mind Reading* (William Ickes, Promethuses)

Happiness:

1. *The Power of Now* (Ekharte Tolle, New World Library)*
2. *Emotionally Free: Letting Go of the Past to Live in the Moment* (David Viscott, MD, Contemporary Books)
3. *The Happiness Project* (Gretchen Rubin Harper)

Perfection:

1. *Happy Without Being Perfect* (Alice D. Domar, PhD, Crown Publishing)
2. *The Gifts of Imperfection* (Brené Brown, PhD, Hazelden Publishing)

3. *Overcoming Perfectionism* (Ann W. Smith, MS, Health Communications)

Acceptance:

1. *The Happiness Trap* (Dr Russ Harris, Exisle Publishing)*
2. *Get Out of Your Mind and into Your Life* (Steven C. Hayes, PhD, New Harbinger Publications)
3. *The Radical Acceptance of Everything* (Ann Weiser Cornell Calluna Press)

God:

1. *A New Earth* (Ekharte Tolle, Doubleday) *
2. *God on Your Own* (Joseph Dispenza, Jossey-Bass)
3. *God without Religion* (Sankara Saranam, BenBella Books)

Boundaries:

1. *Boundaries* (Henry Clour and John Townsend, Zodervan) *
2. *Dealing with the CrazyMakers in Your Life* (Dr David Hawkins, Harvest House Publishers)
3. *The Dance of Intimacy* (Harriet Leaner, PhD, Harper Paperbacks) *

Codependency:

1. *Codependant No More* (Melody Beattie, Hazelden Publishing) *
2. *Facing Codependence* (Pia Mellody, Harper and Row) *
3. *The Language of Letting Go* (Melody Beattie, Hazelden Publishing) *

4. *The New Codependency* (Melody Beattie Simon and Schuster) *

Being Yourself:

1. *Self Within Marriage: The Foundation for Lasting Relationships* (Richard M. Zeitner, Taylor and Francis)
2. *The Journey to Be Your Own Best Friend* (Paula Klee Parish)
3. *Learning to Love Yourself: Finding Your Self-Worth* (Sharon Wegscheider-Cruse, Health Communications, Inc.)

Self-Esteem:

1. *The Courage to Be Yourself: A Woman's Guide to Emotional Strength and Self-Esteem* (Sue Patton Thoele, Congari Press) *
2. *Claiming Your Self-Esteem: A Guide out of Codependency* (Carolyn M. Ball, Celestial Arts)
3. *Loving the Self-Absorbed* (Nina W. Brown, New Harbinger Publications)

Alone vs Lonely:

1. *Living Alone and Loving It* (Barbara Feldon, Fireside)
2. *The Art of Being a Woman Alone* (Florence Falk, Three Rivers Press)
3. *Living Single in a Double World* (Marjorie Barton, CeShore Publishing Co.)

Thoughts:

1. *Your Body Believes Every Word You Say* (Barbara Hoberman Levine, Words Work Press)

2. *Choose Them Wisely: Thoughts Become Things* (Mike Dooley, Atria Books)
3. *Power Thoughts* (Joyce Meyers, Faithwords)
4. *Experience for Good Now!* (Louise L. Hay, Hay House)

Control:

1. *The Control Freak* (Les Parrott III, PhD, Tyndale House Publishers, Inc.)
2. *Too Perfect: When Being in Control Gets out of Control* (Allan E. Mallinger, MD, and Jeanette Dewyze, (Random House Publishing)
3. *The Dance of Connection* (Harriett Learner, Harper Paperbacks)*

Wisdom:

1. *Why Don't We Listen Better?* (Jim Petersen, Petersen Publications)
2. *.Finding Wisdom* (Merriam Fields Bleyl, Xlibris Corp.)

Enjoy:

1. *The Secret* (Rhonda Byrne, Atria Books)
2. *The Gift of Time* (Alexander Anderson, TMPress)
3. *The Life You Were Born to Live* (Dan Millman, H.J. Kramer)